Prayer, God's Answer

by

Samuel J. Barone III

Prayer, God's Answer

By Samuel J. Barone III

Copyright © 2014

ISBN 13: 978-0692911099 (Samone Publications)

ISBN 10: 069291109X

Lord, Make My Life Matter

Through the need and the pain,

The suffering and the gain,

Through prosperity or financial lack,

Through the joy or spiritual attack,

Lord, make my life matter.

Make my life matter.

More than my praise and thanksgiving,

More than any earthly living,

More than my desire to please You,

Even more than the love I offer You,

Lord, make my life matter.

Make my life matter.

It is far greater to turn to the mercy

Of a living, loving God,

Than to remain chained forever to the darkness,

Blinded to His grace.

Acknowledgements

It would only be fitting that I first acknowledge the one who is first in my life. Without my Lord, Jesus, and the inspiration from His Holy Spirit, this book would have never been imagined let alone conceived. Therefore, I am grateful for the opportunity to have authored this book, yet the credit is all His.

However, as we all know, the Spirit of God uses people to accomplish His will. I would like to acknowledge the following precious souls for the planting, watering, and waiting patiently while the seeds of life and deliverance grew during the writing of this book.

My wife, Peggy, whose kind words of peace and wisdom are like gentle whispers from heaven, always spoke at just the right time. She has always been my priceless gem. She is God's constant reminder to me of His everlasting love for even the most wretched of men – of which I once was too.

My pastor, Joshua Williamson, saw the Spirit of God moving in me when I could not. As all good pastors, he was like an eagle pushing its chick out of the nest at the precise moment to fly. Kicking and screaming in my spirit, I cried, "No, I will not!", when he asked me to teach a Sunday morning course on prayer. Of course, I eventually agreed to his request. It is a funny thing how the Spirit of God showed up every morning during the week in my devotions and before those Sunday classes. One day, I might get with the program and just drop the drama…we'll see.

My former pastor, Mark Turansky, made me laugh when he suggested I take the notes from the course on prayer and consider writing a book on the subject. Now I know how Abraham's wife, Sarah, must have felt when she laughed after God promised her a child – "Yeah right, Lord!" I'm not laughing now. Is anything too great for our God to do?

My good friend Donna (MelloDe) DeMello painstakingly worked on the first draft of this manuscript. May God's richest blessings fall continually upon her for her boundless patience and literary skill. It was amazing to see God work through her to make something out of nothing. However, it was truly a blessing for me to see how God used her faithfulness to open her heart while she edited the manuscript and pondered the biblical principles contained in it.

My good brother, Chris Baggett, has blessed me with his professionalism and photographic skills to help create the book's cover. No clip art or stock photographs here!

My wonderful sister in the Lord, Val Horne, provided outstanding simplistic yet sophisticated graphic designing skill on the book's cover.

Then there were numerous brothers and sisters from my church who gave their endless encouragement to finish the race and be obedient to God by completing this book.

And then there is my mother, Shirley, who chose life and birthed me…need I say more?

Dedication

This book is dedicated to my brother, Scott, whose heart thirsts for the One whose voice cries out to him. I pray he recognizes Jesus' voice and answers His cry (1 Samuel 3:1-21).

A Special Note from the Author

Have you ever believed you had a firm understanding of something, such as prayer, and then realized that there was so much more? I did. For example, If God is all powerful, all knowing, everywhere all the time, then why pray? Does He not know our needs even before we ask Him? Another question to consider: does God answer or even hear all our prayers, truly hear all of them? If your identity is in Christ, then who are you and what does that have to do with prayer? If you think you know the answers to these questions, how confident are you in them? On the other hand, maybe you have never asked yourself these questions and realize how important the answers are. Come join me on a journey through the Bible that I pray will open your spiritual eyes to prayer and a deeper walk with Christ!

Possibly, like many others, you are not a Christian. Maybe you believe God has failed you or He is not worthy of your trust. Perhaps, on the other hand, you believe you have failed God and are not worthy of His forgiveness. Could it be that you believe you cannot forgive yourself?

The fact is, once someone has heard the truth, only a lie can keep him or her from the love of God. This book contains truth, because within it is the Word of God, which is its foundation. It points to and walks the reader through the Word of God. However, only the Spirit of God can reveal the Word of God and give life to the reader.

A Christian is a person who has come to the point in his or her life where they understand that apart from God everything is meaningless. When one turns away from the futile effort of trying to make life work and turns to *the One* who created all that we can experience here on this planet, they find Jesus. Only through Jesus can we find true meaning to life. It is through Jesus that we become children of God and begin to taste how great the Father's love is for us.

God's message to you and to me is so simple even children can understand it. God is good, and He desires to be active and part of our life, part of who we are. God created people with a free will and the ability to choose: to choose good or evil, life or death, and to obey or disobey. It was because of this free will that Adam and Eve disobeyed God and fled from the Garden of Eden. The bad news is that we are born into a world that is cursed with death because of that choice of disobedience to God. This disobedience plagues us even today. This disobedient foundation of our human condition is our desire toward sin—to choose what we want when we want it. However, the good news is this same free will also makes it possible for us to choose the gift of redemption through God's grace, a redemption that restores us back to the relationship we had with God our Father at the beginning. Only this time, it's better!

Like all gifts, God's grace is free. You cannot earn it, you do not deserve it, but you do have to receive it. How do we receive God's free gift of grace, which saves our souls? It is by asking for and accepting forgiveness for our disobedience. This forgiveness that makes us right with God is only found in Jesus. Without Jesus, we are held captive in a world separated from God.

It is through Jesus and the price He paid that ransomed us back to our Heavenly Father. God became a man because of His indescribable love for each one of us by providing Himself as the only pure sacrifice acceptable to a Holy God. Yes, Jesus became a man, but He has always been God. Confused? That's ok, it's called faith! We will discuss that further.

If you have come to a place in your life where you are tired of living a lie and realize you are broken and in need of fixing, that is good. If you realize there is nothing you can do to change this, apart from God, this is even better! So why not lay it all down and turn it over to the One who has been waiting for you even before you were in your mother's womb?

The Bible says "today" do not harden your heart.

"Today, if you hear his voice,

do not harden your hearts

as you did in the rebellion."

– Hebrews 3:15

Do you know why it says "today"? Sure you do, because there may not be a tomorrow! Let today be your "today." Pray this prayer with me:

"O God, Creator of heaven and earth and all that is, I know there is no God but You. However, I do not know You. I realize my life is meaningless without You, that I am dead without You. I choose this day, today, to walk away from my sin, to renounce all that is displeasing to You. I want my ways to be Your ways. I want Your love in my life. I believe You,

Jesus, are God, who became a man and died for me, to pay for my sin and ransom me back to the Father. I accept You as my Lord, as my Savior, as my King, and Your promise of eternal life with You. Fill me with Your Holy Spirit so that I may walk in Your ways and be the joy in Your eyes, forever and ever. I pray this in the authority of my Great High Priest and Your Name, Jesus. AMEN!"

So be it! If you prayed that prayer with me, it is decreed on a scroll in heaven where it will remain forever. You are now a child of the living God and of our Savior, Jesus Christ. Nothing can change that. The demons of hell cannot and the angels of God will not!

Now this is very, very important. The Bible says:

If you declare with your mouth, "Jesus is Lord," and believe in your heart that God raised him from the dead, you will be saved. – Romans 10:9

Therefore, tell someone that you have just given your life to Jesus Christ. Share your joy with a fellow believer in your first act of obedience as a Christian. God's richest blessings will continually fall upon you like showers from heaven. Although we may never meet on this side, I love you, my brother or sister.

Thank you for blessing my soul.

- Sam

See you on the other side.

Arrayed in splendor,

On bended knees,

Let us render

Crowns of glory

Offered at the feet of Jesus!

\- Written by the Author

Forward

A tale is told about a small town that had historically been "dry," but then a local businessman decided to build a tavern. A group of Christians from a local church were concerned and planned an all-night prayer meeting to ask God to intervene. It just so happened that, shortly thereafter, lightning struck the bar and it burned to the ground. The owner of the bar sued the church, claiming that the prayers of the congregation were responsible, but the church hired a lawyer to argue in court that they were not responsible. The presiding judge, after his initial review of the case, stated that "no matter how this case comes out, one thing is clear. The tavern owner believes in prayer and the Christians do not."

Do you believe in prayer? Many of us say we do, but our actions do not line up with our beliefs. In a recent survey at our church, 45% of our church congregation described their prayer life as "frustrating, mediocre or hit and miss."

Sam Barone takes us on a journey to help Christians regain their belief in prayer – beliefs that line up with practical results that can lead to a more connected and intimate relationship with God. From the basics of prayer theology to common questions about prayer, Sam takes the reader on a guided journey that culminates in a how-to-pray guide that will transform you, your church, and those whom God brings you into contact with.

This guide, along with your Bible and the power of the Holy Spirit, can bring new vitality to your prayer life. Prayer is something nobody is born an expert at it; no one ever masters it. However, we need to learn, and that is what this study guide will help you do.

"Lord, teach us to pray." – Luke 11:1(b)

My prayer for the reader: Father, help us to overcome the barriers that are keeping us from enjoying the benefits of prayer and relating to You. Lord, teach us to pray. In Jesus' name, Amen.

Pastor Mark Turansky

Pacific-Islands Bible Church

Author of *Figure it, Face it & Fix it*

2015

Table of Contents

Chapter 1
Introduction to This Prayer Guide

Like a commander of a stealthy submarine armed with powerful missiles, Jesus' masterful deployment of questions sought out their target and struck with precision. Jesus' use of questions stimulated active learning, cutting deep into one's heart.

━━━◆━━━━━━━━━━━━━━━━━━━◆━━━

Have you ever asked yourself the following questions: What does the act of praying do in my life? How is the act of praying drawing me closer to Jesus?

Have you ever prayed for someone or something only to receive an answer that was totally the opposite of what you believed was God's answer or perhaps you never saw an answer to your prayer? Let's say you were praying for someone's healing and God chose to bring that loved one home to heaven instead. You may have prayed for a financial miracle and the next day lost your job. You may have prayed for your daughter's salvation and, instead of running into the arms of Jesus, she chose to run away from home because she was pregnant. Does it seem the more you pray the more frustrated you are with the results of your prayers? Could it be that the effect of your "act of praying" causes changes within you that are greater than what you could achieve by having your prayers answered as you thought they should?

Have you ever struggled with questions referring to who God is, who Jesus is, or even who you are? Despite being a Christian for many years, recurring questions surface, such as why do I seem to always miss it when I try so hard to do the right thing? Or why do I seem to battle the same destructive patterns in my life? Why do we go through life's challenges seeking permanent answers on our own, only to find, in the end, a temporary solution or the frustrating reality of knowing our efforts are eventually in vain? Why are we compelled to seek answers in our own strength to life's most perplexing questions when it is obvious that God will provide the answers?

Our nature as human beings are to fix things—or at least have the desire to fix things because we are "broken." We must come to grips with the reality that we cannot fix ourselves, despite the many resources available, without God's guidance and help. Any attempt toward true healing, prosperity, peace, love, joy, salvation, or redemption apart from God is, well, *apart from God*!

Why do we often enter into prayer as the last resort, last hope, or when we think all hope is lost? Moreover, when we do pray, we focus so intently on *our* answer to the prayer that we miss what God is truly doing in our life. Many Christians find themselves consumed with believing that God will answer prayer *their* way that their faith is in peril of shipwreck when they don't see the answer they believed God would provide. Without a change of course, they are doomed.

I believe the Spirit of God has inspired this book. The hours of prayer and meditation on the Holy Scriptures, journaling, fasting, and consulting with those I respect as having a close walk with Christ has led me to believe that the preparation for this guide was sufficient. When I reviewed the manuscript prior to submission to the copyeditor, I realized that I simply penned the truths, not invented them. It is therefore my hope and prayer that the Holy Spirit of God draws and captivates everyone who opens this book and reads these words. I pray that the revelation received by the reader will result in such an overwhelming thirst and hunger for God, for God's Word, and for Jesus that they will have difficulty putting their Bible down. I pray that this guide is a reference and a tool to understand the power of prayer in every believer's life, with the ultimate goal of growing closer to Jesus.

I wrote this study guide on prayer to challenge the reader to consider the following:

1. Answer to prayer is God's domain. We are responsible to ensure that we offer up our prayers to the Holy One according to His will with a pure and undivided heart, in faith.

2. And it is through spiritual discipline, such as prayer and the study of the Holy Scriptures, that we find the true answers to life's struggles, our identity, and God's individual purpose for each of us.

In doing so, I pray that God's awesome grace will cause you to find true awareness of who you are, of who you are created to be in His image of you in Christ Jesus, our Lord and Savior, our King Eternal, and the everlasting God.

This guide will unlock the power, joy, and excitement of prayer in one's life. However, God will do much more when we open our hearts to others and learn together. God loves to see brothers dwell in unity. There are things that we can only learn about our Heavenly Father and ourselves corporately, with other brothers and sisters in Christ. Often, the Spirit of God will use the most unlikely of individuals, even the lost, to teach us and help us grow closer to Christ.

This guide to prayer can be used in your personal devotion time. I have also used these principles very effectively at my church on Sunday mornings as a course on prayer before services. It can be used as a Bible study after school with classmates or during home schooling as part of an overall curriculum. It can be used individually in the morning and then discussed as a family during or after dinner.

I personally love the weekly gathering in a home. As the host, you can exercise your abilities of hospitality, leadership, and teaching. We would take turns opening our homes as facilitators, sharing and giving each other the responsibility and opportunity for mentoring and discipleship. We had wonderful times of pouring ourselves into each other, receiving from each other, growing together, and experiencing the faithfulness of the Spirit of God.

I have not even begun to discuss how this guide to prayer can be used as an evangelical means to reach out to those in need and to relate it to those in the community who are ripe for the harvest. Yes, I am referring to those in our family, people we work with, and our neighbors. Everyone has questions about prayer. The saying "there are no atheists in a foxhole" is true. Even the consensus among our scientific and medical community has concluded that prayer is effective. They just do not know why or how, but we do!

Ideally, this guide to prayer was designed to instruct groups between 6 and 10 people, but I have used it effectively for a group greater than 25 people. Remember, this is a study guide designed to help people actively learn about prayer. When used within a group, it is extremely important that everyone have time to share and participate. This is where true learning begins. This is why Jesus taught to groups of people, He taught in parables, and He asked multitudes of people questions. Have you ever counted how many questions Jesus asked while teaching others? One source listed 135 questions asked by Jesus in the New Testament.

We know Jesus did not ask those questions for His own benefit. Like a commander of a stealthy submarine armed with powerful missiles, His masterful deployment of questions sought out their target and struck with precision. Jesus' use of questions stimulated active learning, cut deep into one's heart, and are still one of the most, if not *the* most, effective teaching techniques available to us.

The purpose of this guide is to gain a better working understanding of prayer through asking questions and going to the Holy Scriptures for the answers. In doing so, you will be better equipped to pray and use prayer the way God intended. How will this guide to prayer do that?

First, we must talk about Whom we pray to. It is our nature to want to jump right in to the mechanics of prayer. The crowd asked Jesus, *"Lord, teach us to pray" (Luke 11:1).*

Why? Because we want answers to our prayers, and we want them now! We live in a world demanding instant gratification and our nature is a byproduct of that. However, when we go into prayer and make our requests known, do we really stop and think about what we are asking and to Whom we are asking it from?

If we are going into prayer wanting answers from God, we must first ask ourselves: who is God? In addition, who is Jesus? Moreover, if we are willing to seriously ponder these two questions, honestly and thoroughly, we must be willing to consider the next logical question: who am I?

Did you know, as Christians, we have certain responsibilities? Did you know, the only way to exercise your responsibility as a Christian is to walk in your divine authority and power? Did you know, not understanding how to walk in divine authority and power has caused many godly Christians to shipwreck their faith? Knowing this is essential to understanding who we are and our purpose on this earth—and that is no joke. My brothers and sisters, this is serious business; this is God's business! When we understand that prayer is more, so much more, than getting answers to prayer, then we can move on to the mechanics of prayer, and we will!

We will discuss why we pray, why we do not pray, and how to pray. We will also wrestle with the question: does God answer or even hear our prayers?

Lastly, we will ask the questions: Is doing the will of God difficult or easy? Moreover, what does that have to do with prayer?

As we discussed above, this guide is based on the teaching method of asking questions. After each chapter, you will receive an assignment to do the following:

1. Review the questions for the next chapter, and write down your answers to the questions based on your current understanding.

2. Before reading the next chapter, pray and try to search the Holy Scriptures for biblical answers to these questions. Write down the Holy Scripture references, take notes, and answer the questions based on your biblical understanding.

3. Read the chapter and compare these answers (your preliminary answers and your answers based on your search of the Bible) with the answers in this guide to prayer.

4. At the group study, listen to others and share what you have learned. Soon, you will see what and how much the Spirit of God has revealed to you! You will be amazed at how much you will grow using this guide daily in your life and through the fellowship of others.

When it comes to asking questions we, especially those in the western world, want very clear answers. However, often with the things of God, the answer itself is a mystery. It is the quest for those answers that gives birth to the more important pursuit of God. It is through the *quest* that more *quest*ions are born and more revelation obtained. It is through this quest that our appetite and desire for more of God and more of Jesus grows.

Welcome to a journey that will change your life forever as you grow closer to Christ and bless God, our Father.

This Chapter's Prayer for You

Father God, thank You for touching the heart of Your beloved child and giving them a thirst and hunger for more of You. I pray that You well up an expectancy and excitement for what You are about to do in them through Your Holy Spirit as they search their heart and Your Holy Scriptures for the answers that bring eternal life. Teach us and reveal to us, O God, who You really are! We pray this in the wonderful name of Jesus.

God the Father's Promise to You

"You will seek me and find me when you seek me with all your heart." – Jeremiah 29:13

Questions for Next Chapter

1. Who is God?
2. What does that have to do with prayer?

Chapter 2
Who Is God?

The qualities of God do not define God; God defines His qualities!

―――――――――――――――――――――――

This Chapter's Questions

1. Who is God?
2. What does a biblical understanding of who God is have to do with prayer?

What has God shown you so far in preparing for this chapter after reviewing these questions?

The Bible starts at the beginning of time:

"In the beginning God created the heavens and the earth. Now the earth was formless and empty, darkness was over the surface of the deep, and the Spirit of God was hovering over the waters. And God said, 'Let there be light,' and there was light. God saw that the light was good, and he separated the light from the darkness. God called the light 'day,' and the darkness he called 'night.' And there was evening, and there was morning—the first day." – Genesis 1:1-3

The above passage of Scripture clearly states that God was present before the foundations of the earth, before creation—before light! This light is not the light the Bible is talking about when it says, *"God is light"* *(1 John 1:5)*. That light is beyond our comprehension. That light is unapproachable *(1 Timothy 6:16)*. The word "light" represents God's purity and holiness. As fallen creatures, we can never fathom the depth of God's qualities, let alone who He is *(John 1:9-11)!*

The qualities of God do not define God; rather, God defines these qualities! For example:

Qualities of God	Opposing Quality
He is more than just Light; He is Light	Darkness
He is not just Peaceful; He is Peace*	Evil/War
He is not just Loving; He is Love*	Hate
He is not just Joyful; He is Joy*	Misery
He is not just Patient; He is Patience*	Intolerance
He is not just Kind; He is Kindness*	Cruel
He is not just Good; He is Goodness*	Dishonor
He is not just Faithful; He is Faith*	Fear
He is not just Gentle; He is Gentleness*	Abuse
He is not just Merciful; He is Mercy	Judgement
He is not just Forgiving; He is Forgiveness	Vengeance
He is not just Just; He is Justice	Corrupt

*Galatians 5:22

Consider: is an apple an apple tree? Of course not, and neither should God's qualities be confused with God, the Creator of those qualities. For the Christian, the qualities of God manifest in us as the fruit of the Spirit of God *(Galatians 5:22)*.

In another example, qualities have an opposite and equal counterpart. God has no opposite; God has no equal.

"I am the LORD, and there is no other; apart from me there is no God." – Isaiah 45:5

"I AM that I AM." – Exodus 3:14

Q. Who is God?

Before we can answer this question, we must consider what exists without an equal or opposite.

1. God is sovereign. God is subject to no one or nothing. He is supreme to everyone and everything. *Jesus* is our King of Kings and Lord of Lords *(Revelation 19:16; Philippians 2:9-11; Titus 1:1-3; Hebrews 2:8, 9; 1 Timothy 6:15, 16)*.

2. God is holy. *Jesus* is our Great High Priest *(Hebrews 4:14)*. It was the precious blood of Christ, the sinless, spotless Lamb of God *(1 Peter 1:18, 19, NLV)*.

3. God is His Spoken and Written Word. *Jesus* is the Word of God *(John 1:1-2, 14)*.

4. God is infinite and eternal. Jesus is our Alfa and Omega, our First and the Last (Revelation 1:8,

21:6, 22:13; the end of chapter 1 and all of chapters 2 and 3; 2 Timothy 1:9(b); 1 Peter 1:19, 20).

So, who is God? *Jesus* is God!

Q. What does a biblical understanding of who God is have to do with prayer?

The world is full of people who are searching for God. The problem is that many people don't know it. They look for that most precious of gems, a gem that only God can provide. It is a gem they have never seen before, yet they know deep down inside exists. So, they settle for second best, which never truly satisfies. They do not realize, while looking for silver, that they are digging through a vein of gold, God's gold!

However, as Christians, we *are* looking for gold. The problem for us is recognizing it when we see it, or will we allow "fool's gold" to deceive us? People, brothers and sisters in Christ, I am speaking to those who think they are right with God, but are instead deceived by falsehoods.

As Christians, we often read verses in the Bible without meditating on them. We sometimes neglect the Spirit of God working in our hearts and in our spirit as He tries to impress the gravity of such words in our spirit. *James 4:8*, says, *"Come near to God and He will come near to you."* Is this verse something to take lightly? No!

The Apostle Jude warns, *"For certain men whose condemnation was written about long ago have secretly slipped in among you. They are godless men, who change the grace of our God into a license for immorality and deny Jesus Christ our only Sovereign and Lord" (Jude vs. 4).*

Revelation 3:20 says, *"Here I am! I stand at the door and knock. If anyone **hears my voice** and **opens the door**, I will come in and eat with that person, and they with me."* These are Jesus' words (you know, the ones in the Bible written in red!) to the churches, not to those who are lost in this world. He spoke these words after warning the churches against deception, immorality, deeds (works apart from Christ), idleness, and a hard heart.

Summary

The Apostle Paul wrote, *"What is more, I consider everything a loss because of the surpassing worth of knowing Christ Jesus my Lord, for whose sake I have lost all things. I consider them garbage, that I may gain Christ and be found in him, not having a righteousness of my own that comes from the law, but that which is through faith in Christ—the righteousness that comes from God on the basis of faith. I want to know Christ—yes, to know the power of his resurrection and participation in his sufferings, becoming like him in his death"* (Philippians 3:8-10).

He also said, *"Not that I have already obtained all this, or have already arrived at my goal, but I press on to take hold of that for which Christ Jesus took hold of me. Brothers and sisters, I do not consider myself yet to have taken hold of it. But one thing I do: Forgetting what is behind and straining toward what is ahead, I press on toward the goal to win the prize for which God has called me heavenward in Christ Jesus"* (Philippians 3:12-14).

So, as brothers and sisters in Christ, how do we come (or draw) near to the one and only God?

Knowing who God the Father is through God the Son, Jesus, gives us a *spiritually tangible identity,*[1] which strengthens us through God the Holy Spirit. As we allow the Holy Spirit of God to reveal Jesus to us, we begin to see who *we* are becoming. *"For now we see through a glass, darkly; but then face to face: now I know in part; but then shall I know even as also I am known" (1 Corinthians 13:12, KJV).* We begin to see God's image of us and who we truly are.

We find our *identity* in the Person of God the Son, Jesus Christ—how? It is through spiritual discipline, of which prayer (hearing God's voice) and searching the Holy Scriptures (walking through the door) are paramount *(Revelation 3:20).* And that is why you are here!

In this study, we will find Jesus Christ also as the *Son of Man.* As such, we see the perfect, whole man. As we study Jesus through the Gospels, we see that He gave us an example of how God the Father sees us in a humanity that is perfect (or mature) and unbroken.

Consider and meditate on the following Scriptures:

"Jesus answered: 'Don't you know me, Philip, even after I have been among you such a long time? Anyone who has seen me has seen the Father. How can you say, "Show us the

---

[1] "Tangible" is defined as: to perceive one's environment through the senses; touch, taste, smell, sight, hearing, including the spiritual senses.

Father"? Don't you believe that I am in the Father, and that the Father is in me? The words I say to you I do not speak on my own authority. Rather, it is the Father, living in me, who is doing his work. Believe me when I say that I am in the Father and the Father is in me; or at least believe on the evidence of the works themselves.'" – John 14:9-11

"We know also that the Son of God has come and has given us understanding, so that we may know him who is true. And we are in him who is true by being in his Son Jesus Christ. He is the true God and eternal life." – 1 John 5:20

"I and the Father are one." – John 10:30

Yes, Jesus is God. This is *the* foundational truth and a tenet of our faith as Christians. However, what does this mean? What does this mean to you?

In the following passage, the Apostle Paul is writing to his disciple Timothy about living a holy life. He is talking about God the Father and God the Son, Jesus.

*"I charge you in the presence of God, who gives life to all things, and of Christ Jesus, who testified the good confession before Pontius Pilate, that you keep the commandment without stain or reproach until the appearing of our Lord Jesus Christ, which **He**[1] will bring about at the proper time—**He**[2] who is the blessed and*

*only Sovereign, the King of kings and Lord of lords, who alone possesses immortality and dwells in unapproachable light, whom no man has seen or can see. To **Him**³ be honor and eternal dominion! Amen."* – 1 Timothy 6:13-16, NASV

Who is the Apostle Paul referring to when he uses the pronouns "**He**"¹ (the first time), "**He**"² (the second time), and "**Him**"?³

"**He**"¹ the first time: If you said God the Father, I agree. *"But about that day or hour no one knows, not even the angels in heaven, nor the Son, but only the **Father**"* *(Matthew 24:36).* Here Jesus is speaking about His second coming.

"**He**"² the second time: If you said God the Son, Jesus, I agree. **Jesus** is the King of Kings and Lord of Lords *(Revelation 19:13, 16).*

So then, who is the Apostle Paul referring to when he uses the pronoun "**Him**"?³ If you said, "Huh?", then let's look at what else the Bible says. Throughout the Old Testament of the Bible, we find God referred to many times as the ***Lord God***. For example:

> *"This is the account of the heavens and the earth when they were created, when the **Lord God** made the earth and the heavens."* – *Genesis 2:4*

We also find God referred to as **Lord God** in the New Testament prior to Jesus' birth. For example: *"He will be great* *and will be called the Son of the Most High. The **Lord God** will give him the throne of his father David"* (Luke 1:32). In this passage of Scripture, the angel of God is speaking to Mary and announcing Jesus' birth.

The next place we find the words **"Lord God"** is after Jesus' death in the book of Acts where the Apostle Peter quotes Moses: *"The **Lord God** will raise up for you a prophet like me from your brothers. You shall listen to him in whatever he tells you" (Acts 3:22, ESV).* The Apostle Peter used the words **"Lord God"** only as a reference from the Old Testament.

It is not until the book of Revelation that we see the words *"**Lord God**"* used in the present and future tenses *after* the death of Jesus. Therefore, it appears that the words *"**Lord God**"* is proper *before* and *after* Jesus's life on earth. We do not see the words *"**Lord God**"* used to represent God the Father or God the Son while Jesus walked as a man on the Earth. It was not until the Lamb of God was slain and not until God the Son was reconciled to God the Father that we see the words *"**Lord God**"* used again to represent the *Godhead*, three in one: *God the Father, God the Son, and God the Holy Spirit.*

Jesus *is* God.

This Chapter's Prayer for You

Father God, thank You for the revelation of knowing you are incomprehensible and holy beyond our human ability to attain. You are all powerful, everywhere all the time, and all knowing. Help us to understand that You have made a way for us to have fellowship and grow closer to You through Jesus

Christ as our Lord and Savior. Reveal to us through Your Holy Spirit what that means so that we can begin to walk in the image You have created for us, to see ourselves through Your eyes and to have an identity in Christ that causes us to live a life pleasing to You through Your love! In Jesus' name I pray.

God the Father's Promise to You

> *"So God created mankind in his own image, in the image of God he created them; male and female he created them." – Genesis 1:27*

Questions for Next Chapter

1. What separates Christianity from (and above) every other religion or philosophy?
2. Who is Jesus, and who is Jesus to you?
3. Who are you in Jesus? Hint, answer the question: I am *who*?

Chapter 3
Who Is Jesus?

We are not God and never will be God. However, through the process of sanctification, we obtain true fulfillment and purpose in life because the Spirit of God continues to make us more holy.

———————◆———————

This Chapter's Questions:

1. What (or who) separates Christianity from and above every other religion or philosophy?
2. Who is Jesus? Who is Jesus to you?
3. Who are you in Jesus? (Hint: Answer the question: I am...*who*?)

Q. What (or who) separates Christianity from and above every other religion or philosophy?

Jesus! Must I say any more?

Q. Who is Jesus? Who is Jesus to you?

Everyone will have to answer this question eventually. To some, He was a godly prophet. To others, He was simply a good man. Some people consider Him to have been a charlatan, a master of witchcraft, or a raving lunatic. All of these people have one thing in common, even if they do not realize it. He *was* to them someone from the past.

To the Christian, Jesus was not only someone who *was* from the past, but also someone who *is* and who *is to come.* Concerning Jesus, the Bible says, *"'I am the Alpha and the Omega,' says the Lord God, 'who is, and who was, and who is to come, the Almighty'"* (Revelation 1:8, also 11:17, 16:7, 21:22, 22:6).

To the Christian, Jesus is the Author of our hope, our steadfast Savior, our everlasting Redeemer, our living King, and our only God. To the Christian, there is no exit strategy. There is no plan backed with financial resources in a personal off-shore, secret bank account, "just in case." When someone gives his or her life to Christ, there is no plan B, there is no safety net to fall back *upon except* upon Christ, and that is a good deal! The Bible states it this way:

> *"We wait for the blessed hope—the appearing of the glory of our great God and Savior, Jesus Christ, who gave himself for us to redeem us from all wickedness and to purify for himself a people that are his very own, eager to do what is good." – Titus 2:13, 14*

> *"Now to the King eternal, immortal, invisible, the only God, be honor and glory for ever and ever. Amen." – 1 Timothy 1:17*

So, who is Jesus to you?

Q. Who are you in Jesus?

Complete the sentence: I am ....(*who?*)

Many who are asked this question respond by saying something like: I am a husband or daughter, mechanic or nurse, or wealthy or educated. However, does that define who we are? As Christians, we may answer by saying something like: I am a pastor or teacher or an evangelist or musician. Again, if these answers define who we are, we may be in trouble. For example, if we say we are a mechanic or nurse, then who are we when we retire or are laid off and can no longer continue in our profession? If we say we are a husband or wife, then who are we if our spouse dies or our marriage ends in divorce? If we say we are a pastor or teacher, then who are we when our church is no more? What about the evangelist or worship singer who loses their voice? These are answers to the question *what* we are, but not *who* we are. These are our roles or professions in life. However, *who* we are is a confession that relates to our identity.

Our life is a reflection of who we think we are. Our perception of who we think we are is a choice. A Christian is someone who chooses to believe that he is who God says he is. What does the Bible say about who God says you are? First of all, if you are a Christian, the Bible says you are saved! *"That if you declare with your mouth, 'Jesus is Lord,' and believe in your heart that God raised him from the dead, you **will be** saved' (Romans 10:9).* I described what this means in the section titled "A Special Note from the Author."

As Christians, we understand that God has a plan for our lives. *"'For I know the plans I have for you,' declares the*

Lord, 'plans to prosper you and not to harm you, plans to give you hope and a future" (Jerimiah 29:11). We also understand that the fulfillments of many of those plans require our free will and obedient participation. Yes, God Almighty has a sovereign plan and nothing in heaven or earth, or anywhere else, can change that. However, within His perfect plan, our loving Heavenly Father has given us the choice to walk freely and willingly. When we are presented with the good news of Jesus Christ, we are compelled to choose life or to choose death.

As a Christian, I am who God created me to be. My identity is in Christ Jesus. My identity becomes clearer daily through knowing Jesus. It is through spiritual discipline, such as prayer, meditating on the Holy Scriptures, journaling, fasting, and so on, that the Spirit of God prepares our heart and reveals God the Son, Jesus, more deeply. We are not God and never will be God. However, through this process of sanctification, we obtain true fulfillment and purpose in life because the Spirit of God continues to make us more holy. *"Being confident of this, that he who began a good work in you will carry it on to completion until the day of Christ Jesus" (Philippians 1:6).*

> *"By faith Enoch was taken from this life, so that he did not experience death: 'He could not be found, because God had taken him away.' For before he was taken, he was commended as one who pleased God." – Hebrews 11:5*

In this passage of Scripture, the author is referencing *Genesis 5:24*, where it says that *"Enoch walked faithfully with*

God and then he was no more." What does *"was no more"* truly mean? When we walk with God because we are filled with His Spirit, the image of who we are in Christ Jesus becomes clearer and the perverted image of who we believed we were becomes less.

When Jesus walked this earth among men, He did it as a man. In the Gospels, we see Jesus in His perfect humanity. In the introduction of this book, we discussed how we are born into this world already terribly broken in our humanity because of the sinful nature of this world. One day, the light of the Holy Spirit will completely expose the darkness of this current disorder. His transforming work in us will also re-establish the order that was at the beginning of time in the Garden of Eden. Then we shall be whole and free as the people God created us to be.

Consider and meditate on the following Scriptures:

"Come near to God and He will come near to you." – James 4:8

*As you come to him, the living Stone—rejected by humans but chosen by God and precious to him— you also, like living stones, are being built into a spiritual house to be a **holy priesthood, offering spiritual sacrifices** acceptable to God through Jesus Christ." – 1 Peter 2:4, 5*

So, part of our identity, part of who we are in Christ, is that of a priest: *"But you are a chosen people, a **royal*** *priesthood, a holy nation, **God's special possession**, that you may declare the praises of him who called you out of darkness into his wonderful light" (1 Peter 2:9).*

So, what *is* a priest? As God's priests, we are to represent the people of God, His special possession, before God the Father. As God's priests, we can boldly come before God the Father *(Hebrews 10:19-22)*, before His very throne. Why? Because of the Lamb of God's shed blood, that being Jesus, our great High Priest. Why? To offer spiritual sacrifices acceptable to God *(1 Peter 2:5)*. What are those spiritual sacrifices? We are to offer our crowns of obedience to praise and worship Him and to pray on behalf of His special possession and this lost world! How do we do this? We do this through spiritual discipline and the Spirit of God!

This Chapter's Prayer for You

Father God Almighty, thank You for loving me. I pray that You will reveal Jesus to me through Your Holy Spirit as my Lord, Savior, and King. Give me a thirst and hunger to grow closer to You so that I may walk in Your ways and please You in all I do. Allow me to welcome Your Holy Spirit within my heart and soul so that Your fruit causes meaningful change in me and be abundant for all those in my life who are in need. Reveal to me who Jesus truly is so that I may be who You have truly created me to be. In Jesus' name I pray.

God the Son's Promise to You

"Righteous Father, though the world does not know you, I know you, and they know that you

have sent me. I have made you known to them, and will continue to make you known in order that the love you have for me may be in them and that I myself may be in them." – John 17:25, 26

Questions for Next Chapter

As Christians, we have benefits and responsibilities.

1. What are some of the benefits we have as Christians?
2. What are some of the responsibilities we have as Christians?

Chapter 4
Benefits Yes, but What Are Our Responsibilities as Christians?

To be touched by the living God in our time of need changes our situation forever. To follow Jesus in our time of need changes us forever.

━━◆━━━━━━━━━━━━━━━━━━━━◆━━

This Chapter's Questions

1. What are some of the benefits we have as Christians?
2. What are some of the responsibilities we have as Christians?

What has God shown you so far in preparing for this chapter after reviewing these questions?

Q. What are some of the benefits we have as Christians?

"Praise the Lord, my soul; all my inmost being, praise his holy name.

*Praise the Lord, my soul, and forget not all his **benefits**—*

who forgives all your sins and heals all your diseases,

who redeems your life from the pit and crowns you with love and compassion,

who satisfies your desires with good things so that your youth is renewed like the eagle's."

– Psalms 103:1-5

The benefits of Christ, of being in Christ, and knowing Jesus draws us to our Heavenly Father. King David understood this and continued to say:

"He does not treat us as our sins deserve

or repay us according to our iniquities.

For as high as the heavens are above the earth,

so great is his love for those who fear him;

as far as the east is from the west,

so far has he removed our transgressions from us."

– Psalms 103:10-12

Knowing Jesus as our Lord and Savior has endless benefits. Having a relationship with Jesus means forgiveness, salvation, redemption, healing, and deliverance. Ultimately, knowing Jesus Christ includes eternal life, a peace that passes all understanding, our true identity and purpose in this life, and a freedom from trying to be right with God independent from the Holy Spirit. The benefits are infinite! We receive every one of these benefits through faith in Christ. However, a baseless, blind faith does not engulf us. Our faith is rooted and grounded in knowing that God's faithfulness is evident throughout our life.

> *"Being confident of this, that he who began a good work in you will carry it on to completion until the day of Christ Jesus." – Philippians 1:6*

God's blessings are like kisses from heaven, leaving behind little smudges of lipstick on our checks. We must continue to look for and count those lipstick smudges every day—they are there!

Yes, our faith is not baseless or blind and it is not passive either. Along with the benefits we have as children of the Most High, we have responsibilities. It is through spiritual discipline that we exercise our faith to recall the benefits and blessings of choosing the will of God in our life. This is the secret to greater faith and what the author was referring to when he wrote, *"Now faith is the substance of things hoped for, the evidence of things not seen" (Hebrews 11:1, KJV)*.

Hoping for more of the lipstick smudges that we can see is our evidence for greater kisses from God to come. Simply put, seeing the lipstick smudges are the "visible" evidence that reinforces our faith to trust Him to become an active, integral part of our lives. In other words, when we can't see the hand of God that we so desperately need and our faith is shaken, look for His fingerprints!

Q. What are some of the responsibilities we have as Christians?

Our responsibility in Christ comes from Christ's love for us. Let us first define what responsibility is.

Responsibility (or duty) equals authority and power (righteousness).

For example, a police officer has the responsibility to enforce the law. He carries both a badge (authority) and a gun (power). He carries the authority, represented by the badge, vested in him by a local, state, or federal entity. He carries the power of a gun necessary to execute his responsibility as a duly authorized police officer.

Throughout Jesus' ministry, the religious and eventually government authorities questioned and challenged His authority. We have already studied that Jesus is God and, while He was on this earth, He was also a man.

We see God the Father's love in John 3:16: *"For God so loved the world that he gave his one and only Son, that whoever believes in him shall not perish but have eternal life."*

At that time, Jesus, God the Son, submitted to God the Father because of the love of God. In so doing, He carried out His responsibilities as the Son of God under the authority of God the Father through the power of God the Holy Spirit.

So, why did Jesus do this? Consider the following passage of scripture: *"And a leper came to Jesus, beseeching*

Him and falling on his knees before Him, and saying, 'If You are willing, You can make me clean.' Moved with compassion, Jesus stretched out His hand and touched him, and said to him, 'I am willing; be cleansed.' Immediately the leprosy left him and he was cleansed" (Mark 1:40-42).

During Jesus' life, and at His death, His obedience and love for people bound Himself to the will of God the Father. So in *John 3:16,* we see the love God the Father has for us. Now let's look at God the Son's, Jesus', love for us. Consider *1 John 3:16*: *"This is how we know what love is: Jesus Christ laid down his life for us. And we ought to lay down our lives for our brothers and sisters. "*

Jesus demonstrated His incomprehensible love for us at His *death.* He laid down His life and willfully stretched out His arms to be nailed to that cross. From our perspective, nothing compares to this ultimate sacrifice by Jesus Christ.

> *"But we do see someone who was made a little lower than the angels. He is Jesus, who is crowned with glory and honor because he suffered death, so that by the grace of God he might experience death for everyone.' (Hebrews 2:9) 'But God demonstrates his own love for us in this: While we were still sinners, Christ died for us." – Romans 5:8*

However, I am also challenged to consider how surpassing Christ's love must be for each of us when I reflect upon His *birth*. Jesus Christ set aside His divinity as God to become a man at His *birth*. Yes, God the Creator of Heaven and Earth became a mortal man. At His *death,* He offered Himself to Himself as the only pure and acceptable sacrifice to a Holy God. *"Abraham answered, 'God himself will provide the lamb for the burnt offering, my son'" (Genesis 22:8).* When I consider God the Father's love in *John 3:16,* I also see how surpassing Christ's love must be for each of us in *1 John 3:16.*

As Christians, we have the authority as priests under our Great High Priest, Jesus, to come boldly before the very throne of God. This authority can never be withdrawn or overturned. Our priesthood is similar to the Hebrew priesthood in the Old Testament in that they were born into it through the tribe of Levi. Once born a Levite, always a Levite. Similarly, it is so with our priesthood. God the Father will never overrule our free choice—once a Christian, always a Christian. However, there is a significant difference between Jewish Levitical priests and Christian priests.

The priests under the Levitical priesthood performed their responsibilities as a position. We, however, perform our responsibilities as priests because of who we are, not because of what we do. Our Great High Priest, Jesus, came from the priesthood of Melchizedek. This priesthood line existed before the Levitical Priesthood *(Hebrews 7).* The authority we have from Christ is secure and eternal. As with our salvation, we did not earn our way into this priesthood. There is no sacrifice from within our self which we can offer that will appease our holy God.

"Then he showed me Joshua the high priest standing before the angel of the Lord, and Satan standing at his right side to accuse him.

The Lord said to Satan, 'The Lord rebuke you, Satan! The Lord, who has chosen Jerusalem, rebuke you! Is not this man a burning stick snatched from the fire?' Now Joshua was dressed in filthy clothes as he stood before the angel. The angel said to those who were standing before him, 'Take off his filthy clothes.' Then he said to Joshua, 'See, I have taken away your sin, and I will put fine garments on you.' Then I said, 'Put a clean turban on his head.' So they put a clean turban on his head and clothed him, while the angel of the Lord stood by." – *Zechariah 3:1-5*

As it was with the high priest Joshua, so too has our Great High Priest, the Lord Jesus, snatched us from destruction and took away our sins. It is by His authority and righteousness that compels us to draw boldly before God's throne, His grace and mercy seat. We must humbly come before our Heavenly Father just as we are, broken and filthy because of our willful sin. No amount of self-righteous ceremonial washing can change that.

When we come to Jesus, He sets us free. Through the cleansing power of the Holy Spirit, the hellish, cyclic lies and chains that bind us from being right with God are broken. Then, and only then, can we perform our priestly duties with the authority of God the Father that is found in the love of Jesus Christ.

Our Power (Righteousness) in Christ

Consider and meditate on the following passages of Holy Scripture:

> *"When Jesus saw that a crowd was running to the scene, he rebuked the impure spirit. 'You deaf and mute spirit,' he said, 'I command you, come out of him and never enter him again.' The spirit shrieked, convulsed him violently and came out. The boy looked so much like a corpse that many said, 'He's dead.' But Jesus took him by the hand and lifted him to his feet, and he stood up. After Jesus had gone indoors, his disciples asked him privately, 'Why couldn't we drive it out?' He replied, 'This kind can come out only by prayer.'"* – Mark 9:25-29

The King James Version states it this way: *"And he said unto them, 'This kind can come forth by nothing, but by prayer and fasting'"* (Mark 9:29, KJV).

What was Jesus saying here? That the disciples had not prayed and fasted long enough or hard enough? That they had not used the right prayer formula or fasted from the right foods or things?

Q. Did the disciples have the authority to cast out the unclean spirit? Yes *(Mark 3:14, 15 & 6:7)*.

Q. Did the disciples have the power to cast out the unclean spirit? No.

Q. Why?

Exercising Authority Without Power

Jesus did not rebuke His disciples for attempting to cast out the unclean spirit. Likewise, He will never rebuke us for receiving and exercising the authority we have in Christ. However, He did say, *"'You unbelieving generation,' Jesus replied, 'how long shall I stay with you? How long shall I put up with you? Bring the boy to me'" (Mark 9:19).*

Yes, Jesus was speaking to His disciples on the lack of effect or results of their prayers. Jesus was saying that they did not have the degree of power, or righteousness, or virtue necessary to cast out the unclean spirit. However, the kind of righteousness or virtue that Jesus was speaking about can come only from the Holy Spirit through spiritual discipline, such as prayer and fasting. He was speaking to them of the effect of spiritual discipline on their hearts and growth toward God! *Wow! Take a moment to ponder that!*

What we see from this passage of Scripture is an exercise of proper authority *without* the proper power to enforce proper responsibility. Imagine an authorized police officer walking the beat in a crime-laden area of the city without a gun. He might get away with exercising his authority for a while, but eventually a criminal is going to challenge the police officer's power to enforce his responsibility.

So it is with Christians. As stated previously in this chapter, our responsibility in Christ comes from Christ's love for us. One of the greatest ways we express that responsibility is as Christ's priests. We have the authority as priests of our

Great High Priest, Jesus Christ, just as the disciples had. However, we also need the power to carry out that responsibility. The Bible is not clear when Jesus gave the disciples the authority to use His name, but we know, up until chapter 9 in Luke, they did not possess that particular power. Had they used the name of the Lord in vain? Do you remember the Ten Commandments? Which one is number three? *"Thou shalt not take the name of the LORD thy God in vain; for the LORD will not hold him guiltless that taketh his name in vain" (Exodus 20:7, KJV).*

Therefore, exercising authority without power (righteousness) is accepting responsibility in vain. Why is that a sin? Because we presume to have Christ's righteousness without a relationship with Christ. In other words, we operate in self-righteousness and that is always a sin! Spiritual discipline is the basis of our relationship and growth in Christ.

Exercising Power without Authority

We see many movies where the plot involves a cop who is wrongfully accused of committing a crime. Next, the cop must turn in his or her badge and gun. They always have a backup gun, but now they must clear themselves without a badge, and of course, they always do! In the real world, it rarely works out that way. Imagine a police officer with a gun, but without a badge (authority) to carry out his responsibility. How many police officers do you think are willing to take that chance? If they must use their gun, they may go to jail!

Therefore, power or (self) righteousness without Jesus' authority is irresponsibly reckless, dangerous, and perhaps fatal. Likewise, so it is with Christians. Consider and meditate on the following passage of the Holy Scripture.

> *"Some Jews who went around driving out evil spirits tried to invoke the name of the Lord Jesus over those who were demon-possessed. They would say, 'In the name of the Jesus whom Paul preaches, I command you to come out.' Seven sons of Sceva, a Jewish chief priest, were doing this. One day the evil spirit answered them, 'Jesus I know, and Paul I know about, but who are you?' Then the man who had the evil spirit jumped on them and overpowered them all. He gave them such a beating that they ran out of the house naked and bleeding." – Acts 19:13-16*

Q. Did these Jews have the *power* to cast out evil spirits? Yes, at least initially.

Q. Did these Jews have *authority* to cast out the evil spirit? No, even though they tried to invoke the name of the Lord Jesus.

Q. Why did they not cast out evil spirits in the name of Jesus? These Jews did use the name of Jesus, but they acted in their own authority. Again, we see the disastrous effects of self-righteousness and the eventual price these men paid for their ignorance and presumption.

There are always consequences to self-righteousness under the disguise of God's authority! By using the unauthorized name of Jesus, our actions are irresponsible. This vain exercise of power is self-deceptive resulting in impotent attempts at self-gratification and ultimately grave consequences.

Responsibility Equals Authority and Power (Righteousness).

As Christians, God the Father has given us the *responsibility* to grow closer to Christ because of His love for us. Therefore, we have the *authority* to use the name of Jesus as priests of our Great High Priest, Jesus Christ. As we receive the *righteousness* that comes from the cleansing blood of the Lamb and the *power* of the Holy Spirit, our actions become responsible, effective and avail much.

The author of Hebrews, speaking about our parents, writes, *"They disciplined us for a little while as they thought best; but God disciplines us for our good, in order that we may share in his holiness. No discipline seems pleasant at the time, but painful. Later on, however, it produces a harvest of righteousness and peace for those who have been trained by it"* (Hebrews 12:10, 11).

How do we train ourselves to accept and receive God's discipline? We train ourselves through spiritual discipline (i.e. prayer).

The first half of this study has been on the authority we have as Christ's priests. As we discussed previously, a priest is someone who has the *authority* to approach God's throne of grace on behalf of himself and others.

"But you are a chosen people, a royal priesthood, a holy nation, God's special possession, that you may declare the praises of him who called you out of darkness into his wonderful light." – 1 Peter 2:9

"Let us then approach God's throne of grace with confidence, so that we may receive mercy and find grace to help us in our time of need." – Hebrews 4:16

The remainder of this study is on the righteousness we have in Christ: *"Therefore, confess your sins to each other and pray for each other so that you may be healed. The prayer of a righteous person is powerful and effective" (James 5:16).*

Righteousness comes from Christ's power (virtue).

Consider the following Scripture:

" 'Who touched me?' Jesus asked. When they all denied it, Peter said, 'Master, the people are crowding and pressing against you.' But Jesus said, 'Someone touched me; I know that power has gone out from me.'" – Luke 8:45, 46

Q. Did the woman to whom Jesus was referring ask Him to heal her? No.

Q. Did Jesus knowingly direct His *power* or *righteous* to heal the woman who touched the hem of His garment? No.

Q. Then why did she receive her healing?

I think as Christians we tend to minimize the wonderful works that Jesus did because we see Him as God—and He is! However, we tend to forget that everything Jesus did was as the Son of Man. Everything Jesus did when He walked He did totally reliant and dependent on God the Father. As the Son of Man, Jesus received His power or righteousness when He received the baptism in the Holy Spirit.

> *"Then Jesus came from Galilee to the Jordan to be baptized by John. But John tried to deter him, saying, 'I need to be baptized by you, and do you come to me?' Jesus replied, 'Let it be so now; it is proper for us to do this to fulfill all* **righteousness.**' *Then John consented. As soon as Jesus was baptized, he went up out of the water. At that moment heaven was opened, and he saw the Spirit of God descending like a dove and alighting on him. And a voice from heaven said, 'This is my Son, whom I love; with him I am well pleased.'" – Matthew 3:13-17*

Q. What did Jesus mean when He responded to John and said, *"Let it be so now; it is proper for us to do this to fulfill all* **righteousness**" *(Matthew 3:14, 15)?*

When we walk in the Spirit of God, the power of God is present because of the righteousness or virtue of Christ Jesus. The righteousness Jesus laid down when He became a man was regained when He received the Holy Spirit. The virtue of the Holy Spirit even surpassed the awareness of Jesus when He was a man. In the passage of Scripture above, Jesus was aware that virtue had left Him, but He asked, *"Who touched me?"* For us, this is a wonderful lesson that the power of God, His virtue and righteousness, is for His benefit and purpose, not ours. We cannot direct it, control it, and may not even be aware of it. However, we can rest in Christ, just as Jesus rested in God the Father, knowing that the Spirit of God is active in our life. When we grow in Christ, by moving closer to Jesus through spiritual discipline, the power of the Spirit of God fulfills the will of God the Father. People's lives are touched, many times without even our knowledge. Why? So that God gets the glory!

Therefore, "Let us then **approach** God's throne of grace with **confidence**, so that we may receive mercy and find grace to help us in our time of need" (Hebrews 4:16).

We understand that because of God's incomprehensible love for us and the responsibility we have as Jesus Christ' priests, we can approach God's throne of grace humbly with authority. In addition, we can approach God's throne of grace with *confidence*, because of the *righteousness* we have in Christ. Period! However, we now understand it is through spiritual discipline, such as prayer and fasting, that helps to prepare our hearts so that we can move in the power of the Holy Spirit and draw closer to Jesus.

This Chapter's Prayer for You

Heavenly Father, thank You for allowing me to enter into Your holy presence. You have blessed me as Your child who is called by Your name. I am grateful that You have given me the opportunity and honor to serve as Your priest before

Your throne of mercy and grace. Help me to be faithful and receive this responsibility humbly that I may love You, others, and myself with Your love. Give me a heart for the lost that I may stand in the gap before You on their behalf and bear fruit for Your Kingdom. Teach me to walk in the authority of my Lord, King, and Great High Priest, Jesus Christ and to fulfil Your will through the power of the Holy Spirit. In Jesus' name I pray. Amen.

God the Father's Promise to You

"Therefore, brothers and sisters, since we have confidence to enter the Most Holy Place by the blood of Jesus, by a new and living way opened for us through the curtain, that is, his body, and since we have a great priest over the house of God, let us draw near to God with a sincere heart and with the full assurance that faith brings, having our hearts sprinkled to cleanse us from a guilty conscience and having our bodies washed with pure water. Let us hold unswervingly to the hope we profess, for he who promised is faithful. And let us consider how we may spur one another on toward love and good deeds." – Hebrews 10:19-24

Questions for Next Chapter

1. Are we to pray?
2. If God is omnipresent, omniscient, and omnipotent, then why pray?

Chapter 5
Are We to Pray? Why?

To experience the presence of the Living God and to dwell in His glory is beyond comprehension. To serve Jesus in His holiness with unfettered dominion becomes who we are.

―――――――――――――――――――――――――――

This Chapter's Questions:

1. Are we to pray?
2. If God is omnipresent, omniscient, and omnipotent, then why pray?

What has God shown you so far in preparing for this chapter after reviewing these questions?

Q. Are we to pray?

Please consider the following passage of Scripture:

"Then Jesus said to his disciples: 'Therefore I tell you, do not worry about your life, what you will eat; or about your body, what you will wear. For life is more than food, and the body more than clothes. Consider the ravens: They do not sow or reap, they have no storeroom or barn; yet God feeds them. And how much more

valuable you are than birds! Who of you by worrying can add a single hour to your life? Since you cannot do this very little thing, why do you worry about the rest? Consider how the wild flowers grow. They do not labor or spin. Yet I tell you, not even Solomon in all his splendor was dressed like one of these. If that is how God clothes the grass of the field, which is here today, and tomorrow is thrown into the fire, how much more will he clothe you—you of little faith! And do not set your heart on what you will eat or drink; do not worry about it.'" – Luke 12:22-29.

Q. Is Jesus saying, "There's no need to pray"? How many times does Jesus use the word "worry" or "worrying"?

"Do not be afraid, little flock, for your Father has been pleased to give you the kingdom" (Luke 12:32). Jesus is not saying not to pray; He is speaking about not fearing and having faith!

Answer: Are we to pray? Yes!

Q. If God is omnipresent, omniscient, and omnipotent, then *why* pray?

Through His Spirit, God is:

- Omnipresent – infinite in presence, everywhere, all the time.

- Omniscient – infinite in truth, wisdom, knowledge and understanding.
- Omnipotent – infinite in power.

The reasons we pray:

1. *For* comfort and deliverance in times of crisis *(James 5:13)**
2. For healing (James 5:14-16)*
3. For God's provision (Matthew 6:9-13, 7:7-11)*
4. *For* the Lord to seek and save those who are lost *(Matthew 9:38)**
5. To offer praise and thanksgiving to God because of answered prayer *(Psalm 138:1-3)***
6. To share and demonstrate God's love *(Romans 1:9-12)***
7. To be obedient (1 Samuel 15:22)**
8. To grow closer to God through the prayer of meditation *(Psalm 86:11; Psalm 1:2)***
9. To live peaceful and quiet lives in all godliness and holiness *(1 Timothy 2:1-8)***
10. To conduct spiritual warfare *(Ephesians 6:10-13, 18)***
11. To take hold of *that* for which Christ Jesus took hold of us *(Philippians 3:12)***
12. To Forgive: The Lord's Prayer (Matthew 6:9-13) and Jesus on the Cross**αΩ
13. To be a selfless blessing to God and others *(Psalms 103:1; Romans 1:9-12)***αΩ
14. *For* a stronger faith *(Mark 9:24)**αΩ
15. To be a witness to others of God's goodness and mercy *(2 Corinthians 1:11)***αΩ

NOTE: *When we begin our answer with the word *"for,"* we are really answering the question of *what* are we praying *for? What* are we asking God *for*—such as *for* an answer to a need.

**When we begin our answer with the word *"to,"* we are answering the question *why* do we pray? *Why* we pray is *to do* something or, more specifically, to have something done for us or others.

αΩ Jesus emphasizes special consideration to these aspects of prayer. We will discuss this topic in further detail during in chapter 7 titled, "Does God Hear and Answer All of Our Prayers?"

Our God is a wonderful businessman too! He is in the business of providing us with both products and services!

Q. Why are we to pray?

Because we are Priests of the Most High! *"But you are a chosen people, a **royal priesthood**, a holy nation, God's special possession, that you may declare the praises of him who called you out of darkness into his wonderful light" (1 Peter 2:9).* The most important reason why we pray is because we are priests of the Most High God!

> *"And God has placed in the church first of all apostles, second prophets, third teachers, then miracles, then gifts of healing, of helping, of guidance, and of different kinds of tongues. Are all apostles? Are all prophets? Are all teachers? Do all work miracles? Do all have*

gifts of healing? Do all speak in tongues? Do all interpret?" – 1 Corinthians 12:28-30

The Apostle Paul was speaking about the things, positions of office, and gifts, that God has given the Body of Christ (the church) for order and for the building up of its members. More specifically:

1. The offices of the church: *"So Christ himself gave the apostles, the prophets, the evangelists, the pastors and teachers, to equip his people for works of service, so that the body of Christ may be built up" (Ephesians 4:11, 12).* NOTE: There is no special office of priest in the church!

2. The gifts of the Spirit of God: *"We have different gifts, according to the grace given to each of us. If your gift is prophesying, then prophesy in accordance with your faith; if it is serving, then serve; if it is teaching, then teach; if it is to encourage, then give encouragement; if it is giving, then give generously; if it is to lead, do it diligently; if it is to show mercy, do it cheerfully." (Romans 12:6-8)* NOTE: There is no special gift of the Spirit of God as a priest!

3. The Fruit of the Spirit of God: *"But the fruit of the Spirit is love, joy, peace, forbearance, kindness, goodness, faithfulness, gentleness and self-control. Against such things there is no law" (Galatians 5:22).* NOTE: There is no special fruit of the Spirit of God as a priest!

When we die to this world and live for Christ, we live as His priests!

This Chapter's Prayer for You

Father God, who is like You in all of heaven and earth? There is no one like You. You created all that is. You know every star by name, and yet You care for me, even for every hair on my head. Teach me to pray so that I may grow to know You and Your ways and that I may please You in all that I do. Give me a deep burning desire to walk in Your glory so that I may be Your priest before my Great High Priest, Jesus Christ. Give me a grateful heart willing to serve and praise You in Your presence with joy, no matter what the cost or sacrifice. In Jesus' name I pray!

God the Father's Promise to You

*"But you are a chosen people, a **royal priesthood**, a holy nation, God's special possession, that you may declare the praises of him who called you out of darkness into his wonderful light." – 1 Peter 2:9*

Questions for Next Chapter

1. Why do we *not* pray?
2. What are the legitimate reasons *not* to pray?

Chapter 6
Why Do We *Not* Pray?

To cover our nakedness is what we do. To be vulnerable before God is who we were created to be.

This Chapter's Questions:

1. Why do we *not* pray?
2. What are the legitimate reasons *not* to pray?

What has God shown you so far in preparing for this chapter after reviewing these questions?

Q. What are some reasons why we do *not* pray?

Read the following passages of Scripture and see if you can find the consequences of not praying.

1. *Haggai 1:9-10* – Too busy
2. *1 John 5:21* – Idolatry
3. *1Kings 19:4* – Weariness
4. *Hebrews 4* – Not resting
5. *Luke 12:22-29* – Presumption
6. *Proverbs 6:6-11, 19:24, 20:4, 21:25-26* – Laziness or slothfulness
7. *1 Corinthians 11:28-30* – Ignorance
8. *Hosea 4:6* – Not knowing/realizing how/when to pray

9. *Luke 10:30-37* – Indifference
10. *Luke 10:25-29 and 37* – Not self-righteousness, but love and mercy
11. *I Kings 18:7-9* – Afraid, yielding to fear, no faith
12. *Deuteronomy 8:10-14 and 17* – Ingratitude and pride
13. *Jonah 1:2-3* – Un-forgiveness → disobedience → judgment

Q. What are legitimate reasons NOT to pray?

We must begin to understand who we are in Jesus Christ, how much God the Father truly loves us, how much He desires to be part of our lives, and how He desires to be the center of our attention. By doing so, we will realize there is never a legitimate reason not to come before Him with our petitions, supplications, and intercessions.

> *"Do not be anxious about anything, but in every situation, by prayer and petition, with thanksgiving, present your requests to God. And the peace of God, which transcends all understanding, will guard your hearts and your minds in Christ Jesus." – Philippians 4:6, 7*

So now the real question: does God truly hear and answer all of our prayers?

This Chapter's Prayer for You

Dear Heavenly Father, why is it so hard to pray? Why, at times, am I so prone to carry my anxieties and cares, so reluctant to cast my burdens upon You, Jesus, whose arms are always open? Teach me Your ways, O God, that I may release my faith and trust the rest that is in You, Jesus—a rest and peace that passes all understanding. In Jesus' name I pray!

God the Father's Promise to You

> *"Come to me, all you who are weary and burdened, and I will give you rest. Take my yoke upon you and learn from me, for I am gentle and humble in heart, and you will find rest for your souls. For my yoke is easy and my burden is light." – Matthew 11:28-30*

Questions for Next Chapter

1. Does God *answer all* our prayers?
2. Does God *hear all* our prayers?

Chapter 7
Does God Hear and Answer Our Prayers?

The answers to our prayers are God's domain. The condition of our heart, mind, and the degree of faith we possess are our domain and responsibility.

━━━━━━━━━━━━━━━━━━━━━━

This Chapter's Questions:

    1. Does God *answer all* our prayers?
    2. Does God *hear all* our prayers?

What has God shown you so far in preparing for this chapter after reviewing these questions?

Q. Does God *answer* all our prayers?

> *"Praise the Lord, my soul, and forget not all his benefits." – Psalm 103:2*

Oh how we love to recall the benefits of our loving Heavenly Father and to be called His children. However, embracing the responsibilities that are associated with our walk with Christ may be a different story. Jesus understood this. Early in His ministry, He described these benefits to a lost world. He focused on the love of a Heavenly Father for His children and His desire to bless them—for example the Sermon on the Mount *(Matthew 5:3-10)*.

Consider the following words from Jesus:

> *"Ask and it will be given to you; seek and you will find; knock and the door will be opened to you. For everyone who asks receives; the one who seeks finds; and to the one who knocks, the door will be opened. Which of you, if your son asks for bread, will give him a stone? Or if he asks for a fish, will give him a snake? If you, then, though you are evil, know how to give good gifts to your children, how much more will your Father in heaven give good gifts to those who ask him!" – Matthew 7:7-11*

Jesus gently introduced the need of understanding the responsibilities associated with those called as children of God. He taught using analogies and parables identifiable by the culture at that time. By the end of His ministry, He spoke plainly and clearly to His disciples.

> *"And I will do whatever you ask in my name, so that the Father may be glorified in the Son. You may ask me for anything in my name, and I will do it." – John 14:13-14*

Are Jesus' statements above based in absolute truths or are they conditional truths? The Apostle John addresses this question and described the conditions required for answered prayer.

"Dear friends, if our hearts do not condemn us, we have confidence before God and receive from him anything we ask, because we keep his commands and do what pleases him. And this is his command: to believe in the name of his Son, Jesus Christ, and to love one another as he commanded us." – 1 John 3:21-23

There are conditions to answered prayer, and the Apostle John references our hearts in condemning us.

Q. Is John referring to our conscience when he says, *"If our hearts do not condemn us"*? In other words, is it true to say, "I have peace; therefore, I must be right with God!" On the other hand, is John saying we are right with God when our hearts become pure and undivided?

Q. What is the difference? Can we have peace within and still have an impure heart? Absolutely! When we exercise rationalization and yield to self-deception, we allow our heart to become hard with stubbornness. Therefore, we must not rely on our heart as an instrument for determining our righteousness before God. Our true barometer to gauge the righteousness that comes from Christ is always sensitive to the Holy Spirit of God through spiritual discipline, such as prayer and the Holy Scriptures.

Q. Do you know the difference between being led by your conscience and being led by the Holy Spirit of God? When we are led to make decisions based on our heart's desires, even desires to do good deeds, we risk having our actions condemned before God. The saying "follow your heart" is extremely dangerous, leading to works independent from God. It is only when we yield and submit to the leading of the Holy Spirit that we can rest assured, knowing that our actions please God. *"There is now no condemnation for those who are in Christ Jesus" (Romans 8:1).*

The Apostle James spoke further on this question about answered prayer and described the condition of the heart required for answered prayer: *"When you ask, you do not receive, because you ask with wrong motives" (James 4:2, 3).*

Jesus showed us in the Garden of Gethsemane that He needed help submitting His will to God the Father's. When we seek God's favor and blessings before going to our "Garden of Gethsemane" and asking God for help in submitting our will to His, we risk asking things from God with the wrong motives. (See chapter 9 on "How Do We Pray," Luke 22:39-44, and Matthew 26:36-46 for more information.)

The Apostle James also spoke about another condition to answered prayer and addresses our faith: *"But when you ask, you must believe and not doubt, because the one who doubts is like a wave of the sea, blown and tossed by the wind. That person should not expect to receive anything from the Lord. Such a person is double-minded and unstable in all they do" (James 1:6-8).*

We see that we must meet certain conditions before the Lord honors our prayers, such as a steadfast belief or faith.

"And without faith it is impossible to please God, because anyone who comes to him must believe that he exists and that he rewards those who earnestly seek him" (Hebrews 11:6). However, is the Apostle James saying that if you believe and not doubt that you will receive everything you ask from the Lord? How I wish it were that simple! No, he simply meant that you will not receive what you ask for if you ask without faith.

God will not answer our prayers when we ask without faith in Him! *"And the prayer offered in faith will make the sick person well; the Lord will raise them up. If they have sinned, they will be forgiven" (James 5:15).* What must we have before we can offer up a prayer to God? We must first have the faith to believe in Him for His favor and blessing! How do we obtain the faith to trust in God when we cannot see Him? We must learn to pray for faith! Ah! So now you may say, "So then, if I can't pray without faith, how can I pray FOR faith when I don't have the qualification to pray to begin with—which is faith?"

This is one of the greatest mysteries we will encounter as Christians in this lifetime. Many great theologians have wrestled and pondered this question. It is even at the core of our salvation and the essence of who we are as children of God.

Consider the following passage of Scripture:

Jesus asked the boy's father, "How long has he been like this?" "From childhood," he answered. "It has often thrown him into fire or water to kill him. But if you can do anything, take pity on us and help us." "If you can?" said Jesus. "Everything is possible for one who believes." Immediately the boy's father exclaimed, "I do believe; help me overcome my unbelief!" When Jesus saw that a crowd was running to the scene, he rebuked the impure spirit. "You deaf and mute spirit," he said, "I command you, come out of him and never enter him again." – Mark 9:21-25

Q. Although Jesus rebuked the people present for not believing (Mark 9:19), He did not rebuke the boy's father. Why?

The same story is told in the Gospel of Matthew. In the Apostle Matthew's account, the disciples go to Jesus after this incident. Please consider the following passage of Scripture:

Then the disciples came to Jesus in private and asked, "Why couldn't we drive it out?" He replied, "Because you have so little faith. Truly I tell you, if you have faith as small as a mustard seed, you can say to this mountain, 'Move from here to there,' and it will move. Nothing will be impossible for you." – Matthew 17:19, 20

The boy's father responded to Jesus with very little faith by saying, *"I do believe; help me overcome my unbelief!"* I do not presume to understand the depth of this mystery. Whether we are born with a certain amount of faith or if it is completely God's gift of grace, I don't know. However, I do know that to whatever measure of faith we do possess, it is like a muscle that must be exercised. We must use it or lose it!

This leads us to the second great truth about faith: our faith must be in *Who*, not in what. We have discussed previously that, because of our responsibility as Christians and priests, we have a special relationship with our Great High Priest, Jesus Christ, who is our Lord and King. It is through the love that's found in that special relationship and the power of the Holy Spirit that our faith grows.

How do we pray for faith? We pray for the faith to trust in God and then in His hand of favor and blessing by asking Him to show us His fingerprints upon our life *(Hebrews 11:1)!* We strengthen our faith by asking God to remind us of the times in our life where we believed God for His intervention and He answered our prayers. When you cannot see the hand of God, these are the fingerprints which you must seek!

Let us look at the question of God answering all of our prayers from a different viewpoint. Let's try to answer why God does *not* answer all of our prayers. According to the Apostle James, God will not answer a prayer offered from a doubleminded mentality (meaning without faith or belief) or from an impure heart (wrong motives) *(James 1:6-8; 4:2, 3).*

Consider the following questions:

Q. Is it possible to offer a prayer in steadfast faith but with an impure heart and will God honor that prayer?

Q. Is it possible to offer a prayer with a pure heart but wavering in faith and will God honor that prayer?

Q. Will God honor and answer every prayer offered in steadfast, unwavering faith and a pure, undivided heart?

Hint #1: Is it about the answer to prayer or is prayer the answer?

Hint #2: Jesus in the Garden of Gethsemane.

Q. Does God *hear* all our prayers?

Consider the following passages:

*"If My people, who are called by My name, will humble themselves and pray and seek My face and turn from their wicked ways, **Then will I hear** from heaven and will forgive their sin and will heal their land." – 2 Chronicles 7:14*

*"This is the confidence we have in approaching God: that **if** we ask anything according to his will, **he hears us**. And **if** we know that he hears us—whatever we ask—we know that we have what we asked of him." – 1 John 5:14, 15*

So, does God hear and answer all of our prayers? No! God will not **hear** a prayer offered from an unrepentant, disobedient heart. (Please also see Psalm 51, a prayer from King David's repentant heart.) God will not **answer** a prayer offered in unbelief (a lack of faith or double mindedness) or from an impure heart. Let me say this again: God will not even **hear** a prayer from an unrepentant, disobedient heart. Wow!

Q. Is there ever a reason why the prayers of a "righteous" man are not answered or heard by God?

In other words, does God always honor and answer prayers offered from a repentant heart, with an undivided mind and a steadfast faith? Ultimately, the answers to the prayers of a "righteous" man are *God's domain*, whereas the conditions of our heart, mind, and the degree of faith we possess are *our domain* and responsibility.

This Chapter's Prayer for You

Dear Heavenly Father, thank You for the wisdom that I can come to You in prayer knowing that You love me and desire to answer me with what is best for me. Thank You for the knowledge that You will answer a prayer offered in faith from a pure heart. I understand that You will not suffer a prayer from an unrepentant heart. Help me to offer up my prayer to You with faith and a pure heart according to Your will so that you may hear and answer my prayers. Never cease to remind me that Your answer to my prayer may not be the answer I am looking for and that sometimes no *is* Your answer...thank You God, in Jesus name I pray!

God the Father's Promise to You

*"If My people, who are called by My name, will humble themselves and pray and seek My face and turn from their wicked ways, **Then will I hear** from heaven and will forgive their sin and will heal their land." – 2 Chronicles 7:14*

Question for Next Chapter

1. What are the barriers and hindrances to prayer?

Chapter 8
What Are the Barriers and Hindrances to Prayer?

Even if you were the only one in this world of desolation to look up, Jesus would have still come and died for you.

━━━━━━━━━━━━━━━━━━━━━━━━

This Chapter's Question:

1. What are the barriers and hindrances to prayer?

What has God shown you so far in preparing for this chapter after reviewing this question?

Q. What does Jesus say are the barriers to our prayers and how they hinder our prayers' effectiveness?

The people asked Jesus, *"Lord, teach us to pray"* *(Luke 11:1)*. Jesus first gave us guidance on how to pray with the Lord's Prayer. In Matthew's Gospel, right after *Matthew 6:9-13* (also the Lord's Prayer), we have *Matthew 6:14-34* and *Matthew 7:1-5*. Therein we find the Five F's that Jesus taught us to make prayer effective (or not!).

The Five F's of Prayer: #1 – Forgiveness

"For if you forgive other people when they sin against you, your heavenly Father will also forgive you. But if you do not forgive others their sins, your Father will not forgive your sins." – Matthew 6:14, 15

Consider the following passage of Scripture:

"Jesus stepped into a boat, crossed over and came to his own town. Some men brought to him a paralyzed man, lying on a mat. When Jesus saw their faith, he said to the man, 'Take heart, son; your sins are forgiven.' At this, some of the teachers of the law said to themselves, 'This fellow is blaspheming!' Knowing their thoughts, Jesus said, 'Why do you entertain evil thoughts in your hearts? Which is easier: to say, "Your sins are forgiven," or to say, "Get up and walk"? But I want you to know that the Son of Man has authority on earth to forgive sins.' So he said to the paralyzed man, 'Get up, take your mat and go home.' Then the man got up and went home. When the crowd saw this, they were filled with awe; and they praised God, who had given such authority to man." – Matthew 9:1-8

Q. What is this story about? Is this passage of Scripture about Jesus teaching the "teachers of the law" that

He had the power to forgive sin? Yes, Jesus clearly demonstrates that He had the power to forgive sin by healing the paralyzed man, which He infers is more difficult than to forgive this man's sin. However, Jesus is teaching us a deeper truth.

Q. Who has the power to forgive sin? Yes, Jesus does. Is Jesus the only one with the *authority* and *power* to forgive sin? Read the last verse in the passage above again. *"When the crowd saw this, they were filled with awe; and they praised God, **who had given such authority to man"** (Matthew 9:8).*

Q. What did God give *authority* and *power* to man to do? The "teachers of the law," with their self-righteous mindset of works, is not the same as the works of the Holy Spirit. Because of this mindset, only sin will be seen. As a result, the truth that God the Father, because of God the Son, through God the Holy Spirit, has given the authority and power to man to forgive sin may be missed or overlooked. Jesus, however, focused not on the sin, but on the forgiveness of the sin. Through spiritual discipline and the Holy Spirit's help, we are to release the trespasses committed against us. By doing so, breaches against others caused by these trespasses will be repaired. Now read *Matthew 6:14, 15* again.

Q. Did the paralyzed man ask for forgiveness?

Q. Did his friends intercede for his forgiveness?

Q. In *Matthew 6:14, 15*, did Jesus say that we are to forgive only those who come to us seeking our forgiveness? We have the wonderful *authority* and *power* to forgive even those who do not ask for it— *especially* for those who do not ask for it!

Q. What trespass, or sin, did the paralyzed man commit against Jesus (as a man)? Prior to this event, Jesus taught about forgiveness from a personal perspective. His teaching was about being offended and offending others, about being right with others, and how that affects our prayers *(Matthew 6:14, 15)*. Now we see Jesus addressing a (paralytic) man's sin and unrighteousness toward God, independent of our relationship toward one another. The "teachers of the law" understood this immediately and interpreted Jesus' words as a challenge and threat. They understood what was written: *"When the crowd saw this, they were filled with awe; and they praised God, who had given such authority to man" (Matthew 9:8).* Jesus had exposed their pretense of power through self-imposed authority and self-righteous religion. Jesus was teaching about the true power that comes when we get right with God because of His authority, righteousness and love.

Jesus was proclaiming that He, and those who are His own, not only have the power to forgive the sin committed against oneself, but to forgive the sin committed against God! Regarding this truth, I am absolutely positive that I will not be able to totally fathom the depth of this mystery until I see Jesus. Even then, will I fully understand this aspect of how great God's love and grace truly are? What I do believe with an unwavering, steadfast faith and undivided mind is that, when I meet someone who is ready for the harvest, I can look that person straight in the eyes despite the depth of their sin. I can tell this dear soul that they are precious and profoundly loved by God, that God has a wonderful plan for their life, including a hope and a future with Him, and He will do good things for them. I can tell them that, though their sins may be great, they are forgiven because of the blood of Jesus *(Psalm 51)*.

Yes, they are forgiven in Jesus' name. However, they must receive it. How can I say this with such boldness? I am a child of the Living God and priest of the Great High Priest, Jesus Christ, God the Son. As such, I can come boldly before the Throne of Grace and Mercy offering a prayer of intercession to the Lord of the Harvest on anyone's behalf. *As a Christian, so can you!*

The Five F's of Prayer: #2 – Fasting

Q. Is fasting for today's believer? Consider the following passages of Scripture:

"When you fast, do not look somber as the hypocrites do, for they disfigure their faces to show others they are fasting. Truly I tell you, they have received their reward in full. But when you fast, put oil on your head and wash your face, so that it will not be obvious to others that you are fasting, but only to your Father, who is unseen; and your Father, who sees what is done in secret, will reward you." –
Matthew 6:16-18

Q. What is fasting? Fasting is the action of abstaining from or engaging in something (usually a natural need or desire) in order to receive a spiritual blessing.

Q. Does fasting affect prayer? (How?) Fasting results in clarity of thought because distractions become subject to the Mind of Christ! Fasting is a discipline commanded by God. Fasting slows us down so that we may hear Him!

Q. Why fast? There are several benefits to fasting:

1. Deliverance and provision for others:

"Is this not the fast which I choose, To loosen the bonds of wickedness, To undo the bands of the yoke, And to let the oppressed go free And break every yoke? Is it not to divide your bread with the hungry And bring the homeless poor into the house; When you see the naked, to cover him; And not to hide yourself from your own flesh?" – Isaiah 58:6-7

2. Healing, God's presence:

"Then your light will break out like the dawn, And your recovery will speedily spring forth; And your righteousness will go before you; The glory of the LORD will be your rear guard. Then you will call, and the LORD will answer; You will cry, and He will say, 'Here I am.'" – Isaiah 58:8-9a

3. Deliverance:

"But Jesus took him by the hand, and lifted him up; and he arose. And when he was come into the house, his disciples asked him privately, Why could not we cast him out? And he said unto them, This kind can come forth by nothing, but by prayer and fasting." – Mark 9:27-29, KJV

Q. Why should we fast? Fasting is the spiritual discipline amplifier! It's the discipline that amplifies the effects of other spiritual disciplines, such as prayer and meditation on the Word of God!

The Five F's of Prayer: #3 – First Me (Greed)

"Do not store up for yourselves treasures on earth, where moths and vermin destroy, and where thieves break in and steal. But store up for yourselves treasures in heaven, where moths and vermin do not destroy, and where thieves do not break in and steal. For where your treasure is, there your heart will be also. The eye is the lamp of the body. If your eyes are healthy, your whole body will be full of light. But if your eyes are unhealthy, your whole body will be full of darkness. If then the light within you is darkness, how great is that darkness! No one can serve two masters. Either you will hate the one and love the other, or you will be devoted to the one and despise the other. You

cannot serve both God and money." – Matthew 6:19-24

Q. Which came first, the chicken or the egg? Or which comes first, the evil desires within our heart or the offense of our eyes? In the passage of Scripture above, Jesus exposed the root to the sin of greed (want or lust). He speaks about the wretchedness of this sin leading to the ultimate decision of having to choose between two masters, God and some evil desire in our heart (in this case, the love of money). However, He explained that the root to this sin of greed (want or lust) are unhealthy (spiritual) eyes. Really? Unhealthy (spiritual) eyes are the root to this sin? Yes, they are!

Please consider the following passage of Scripture:

*"In the spring, **at the time when kings go off to war**, David sent Joab out with the king's men and the whole Israelite army. They destroyed the Ammonites and besieged Rabbah. But **David remained in Jerusalem.** One evening David got up from his bed and walked around on the roof of the palace. From the roof **he saw** a woman bathing. The woman was very beautiful, and David sent someone to find out about her. The man said, 'She is Bathsheba, the daughter of Eliam and the wife of Uriah the Hittite.' Then David sent messengers to get her. She came to him and he slept with her. (Now she was purifying herself from her monthly*

uncleanness.) Then she went back home. The woman conceived and sent word to David, saying, 'I am pregnant.'" – 2 Samuel 11:1-5

Q. Did King David, the *"apple of God's eye" (Psalm 17:8),* walk out onto his roof that evening with lust (want or greed) in his heart? Or did he allow darkness to enter his *(spiritual)* eyes when he saw Bathsheba and chose to gaze upon the beauty of another man's wife?

Jesus taught in *Matthew 6:19-24* that it is only a matter of time before the whole body or heart is filled completely with darkness when we choose to lay our *(spiritual)* eyes upon and entertain "treasures" not from God.

Jesus, figuratively speaking, also said, *"And if your eye causes you to stumble, gouge it out and throw it away. It is better for you to enter life with one eye than to have two eyes and be thrown into the fire of hell" (Matthew 18:9).*

The Apostle James elaborated, *"But each person is tempted when they are dragged away by their own evil desire and enticed. Then, after desire has conceived, it gives birth to sin; and sin, when it is full-grown, gives birth to death" (James 1:14, 15).*

There are at least three roots to sin: want (lust or greed), fear (unbelief), and pride. (Please see chapter 8, "Why Is Doing the Will of God Difficult?").

We see the sin of want (lust or greed) enters our hearts through our eyes. We must guard our *spiritual eyes* against the temptation to want (lust or greed). Jesus taught us that the ultimate goal of this sin is to tear us away from our rightful master, God, with a false master of want (lust or greed). When we choose to yield to want (lust or greed), we ultimately say no to God our Father and no longer abide in God the Son, Jesus.

> Q. So how do we break the chains of full-grown sin in our life or, better yet, avoid temptation and rid the seed of sin planted in our heart?

Yes, you guessed it: through *spiritual discipline.* I hope you are beginning to realize how imperative the routine practice of spiritual discipline is to understand and become who we are in Christ and to walk victoriously with Jesus!

The Five F's of Prayer: #4 – Fear

"Therefore I tell you, do not worry about your life, what you will eat or drink; or about your body, what you will wear. Is not life more than food, and the body more than clothes? Look at the birds of the air; they do not sow or reap or store away in barns, and yet your heavenly Father feeds them. Are you not much more valuable than they? Can any one of you by worrying add a single hour to your life? And why do you worry about clothes? See how the flowers of the field grow. They do not labor or spin. Yet I tell you that not even Solomon in all his splendor was dressed like one of these. If that is how God clothes the grass of the field, which is here today and tomorrow is thrown into the fire, will he not much more clothe

you—you of little faith? So do not worry, saying, 'What shall we eat?' or 'What shall we drink?' or 'What shall we wear?' For the pagans run after all these things, and your heavenly Father knows that you need them. But seek first his kingdom and his righteousness, and all these things will be given to you as well. Therefore do not worry about tomorrow, for tomorrow will worry about itself. Each day has enough trouble of its own." – Matthew 6:25-34

Q. What is this passage of Scripture about? (Hint: How many times does Jesus use the word "worry" or "worrying" in these nine verses?)

Q. Why did Jesus teach us not to worry? What is the root to worrying, if not fear? What is the root to fear, but a lack of faith?

Jesus taught us in *Matthew 6:19-24* and in our example about David and Bathsheba that the root to the sin of greed (want or lust) are unhealthy eyes. We see next in *Matthew 6:25-34* that Jesus taught us that the root to the sin of fear (and worry) are unhealthy eyes and a weak mind because of a lack of faith.

In *Matthew 6:25-34*, Jesus taught us to shift our focus (unhealthy eyes) away from worry and the senseless struggle (a weak mind) against daily cares that we have no power over to seeking what pleases God the Father first, His Kingdom, and His righteousness. We have discussed in previous chapters that self-righteousness is the act of trying to do in our own strength what is right apart from God. We have also compared self-righteousness to the righteousness that comes only from our Heavenly Father above. This righteousness consists of His authority and power, both of which come only by faith in Christ Jesus through the Holy Spirit of God. *"And without faith it is impossible to please God" (Hebrews 11:6).*

We understand that a lack of faith in our heart gives way to fear through what we allow our eyes to focus on. Once our eyes are weakened and unhealthy because of an undisciplined heart, fear becomes deeply rooted. It mesmerizes and eventually captivates the heart of its victim, like all sin. However, for the believer, this poor and wrenched human condition of ours need not prevail. *"So then faith comes by hearing, and hearing by the word of God" (Romans 10:17).* When we shift our eyes and ears onto the Word of God, our faith is stirred. The Spirit of God then has the tangible Word of God as tinder to ignite flames within our spirit. Then our hearts are free and our eyes are full of the light of the Spirit of God!

The Five F's of Prayer: #5 – Findings (Judgment - I find you guilty!)

> *"Do not judge, or you too will be judged. For in the same way you judge others, you will be judged, and with the measure you use, it will be measured to you. Why do you look at the speck of sawdust in your brother's eye and pay no attention to the plank in your own eye? How can you say to your brother, 'Let me take the speck out of your eye,' when all the time there is a plank in your own eye? You hypocrite, first*

take the plank out of your own eye, and then you will see clearly to remove the speck from your brother's eye." – Matthew 7:1-5

Please consider the following passage of Scripture:

"'Go to the great city of Nineveh and preach against it, because its wickedness has come up before me.' But Jonah ran away from the Lord and headed for Tarshish. He went down to Joppa, where he found a ship bound for that port. After paying the fare, he went aboard and sailed for Tarshish to flee from the Lord." – Jonah 1:2-3

Q. Why did Jonah flee from the Lord?

"When God saw what they did and how they turned from their evil ways, he relented and did not bring on them the destruction he had threatened." – Jonah 3:10

"But to Jonah this seemed very wrong, and he became angry. He prayed to the Lord, 'Isn't this what I said, Lord, when I was still at home? That is what I tried to forestall by fleeing to Tarshish. I knew that you are a gracious and compassionate God, slow to anger and abounding in love, a God who relents from sending calamity. Now, Lord, take away my life, for it is better for me to die than to live.'" – Jonah 4:1-3

Q. Even though Jonah witnessed firsthand the mercy and compassion of God, he was still angry with God. Why? Jonah had a very deep-seated hatred for the Assyrians who had oppressed Jonah and his people. The Assyrians were part of a great nation at that time and were greatly feared for their ruthlessness and cruelty. Jonah allowed that fear to fester into a personal hatred because he judged the Assyrians as evil and unworthy of God's mercy and compassion.

Q. Why must we never let judgment gain a foothold into our heart? Like vengeance, judgment is sacred and belongs to God *(Romans 12:19)*. When we harbor judgment, we embrace the sin of pride and an unrepentant heart. Judging others is the ultimate expression of self-righteousness.

Q. How can we love and pray fervent, effective prayers with a steadfast faith and an undivided pure heart, yet harbor judgment toward our neighbor *(I John 4:20, 21)?*

Summary

God will not answer a prayer offered in unbelief (a lack of faith) or from an impure heart. God will not even hear a prayer from an unrepentant heart. God will hear and answer *every prayer (Matthew 18:19-20)* when we pray with faith and a pure heart according to His will. It's important to remember that God's answer to our prayer may not be the answer we are looking for and that sometimes no *is* God's answer...thank God!

Are there barriers that hinder our prayers toward God or that temporarily hinder His answers for us, even when we pray with faith and a pure heart according to His will? Absolutely!

1. **Spiritual forces of evil in heavenly realms** *(Daniel 10:12-13; Ephesians 6:12)*. Yes, be not deceived. There is a spiritual battle raging. We must decide if we are going to allow ourselves to be a casualty in this war or if we are going to be part of the victory. Spiritually speaking, there is no innocent collateral damage, only ignorant fatalities or conquerors in Christ. You must choose this day life or death *(Joshua 24:15)*.

2. **Breaches in relationships.** *"Husbands, in the same way be considerate as you live with your wives, and treat them with respect as the weaker partner and as heirs with you of the gracious gift of life, so that nothing **will hinder your prayers**" (1 Peter 3:7)*. And *"Husbands, love your wives and do not be harsh with them" (Colossians 3:19)*. Why? Our God is a God of relationships. The way we treat our neighbors (yes, spouses too) is serious business to God. And who is your neighbor? Ask the Good Samaritan *(Luke 10:29-37)*. We are to love God first and love our neighbor next. There is no greater commandment *(Mark 12:30, 31)*.

This Chapter's Prayer for You

Dear Heavenly Father, help me to develop a prayer life that births peace, wisdom, and the trust that honors You out of a pure heart. Cleanse me of selfish motives that result in barriers that hinder me from a healthy prayer life. I want my desires to be Your desires. Help me to grow my faith by remembering and seeing Your fingerprints upon my life when I cannot find Your hand. Heavenly Father, keep me from an unbelieving, impure and unrepentant heart. Help me to offer up my prayers to You with faith and a pure heart so that You will hear and answer my prayers. Never let me forget that Your answer to my prayer may not be the answer I am looking for and that it's okay when no answer is Your answer. Thank You, Father God, in Jesus' name I pray.

God the Father's Promise to You

> *"And he said, "Abba, Father, all things are possible for you. Remove this cup from me. Yet not what I will, but what you will." – Mark 14:36, ESV*

Questions for Next Chapter

1. Is doing the will of God difficult or easy?
2. Why do I continue to miss opportunities to pray?
3. Why is my prayer life so weak at times?

Chapter 9
Why Is Doing the Will of God Difficult?

Living for Jesus is like running a race you have already won, yet how big will your trophy be?

This Chapter's Questions

1. Is doing the will of God difficult or easy?
2. Why do I continue to miss opportunities to pray?
3. Why is my prayer life so weak at times?

What has God revealed to you so far in preparing for this chapter after reviewing these questions?

Q. Why is doing the will of God difficult?

Doing the will of God, specifically walking in the will of God, is a mystery to many people. However, one thing is certain: to be successful, you must be willing to take a stand for God and get out of His way when it is time. The timing is so crucial. But why is it so difficult to get out of God's way? We will discuss this in more detail latter in this chapter, but the short answer is sin!

To understand what sin looks like, let's look at Psalm 23, verses 1-4. See how wonderful the Psalmist, King David, describes the three areas of victorious rule over sin and a life of righteous, holy living that is available to us!

Psalm 23

Vs. 1-2 Gratitude/Contentment

*The Lord is my shepherd; **I shall not want.***

He makes me lie down in green pastures.

He leads me beside still waters.

Vs. 3 Dependency on God

***He** restores my soul.*

***He** leads me in paths of righteousness*

for his name's sake.

Vs .4 Faith

Even though I walk through the valley of the shadow of death,

I will fear no evil,

for you are with me;

your rod and your staff,

they comfort me.

We see in *Psalm 23* that the three causes of sin are want (lust, greed), pride, and fear. We also see that gratitude and contentment, dependency on God, and faith are the antidotes to such conditions. (Please see chapter 7, "Does God Hear and Answer Our Prayers" and chapter 10 "How Do We Pray?".)

Q. Why do I continue to miss opportunities to pray?

Again, the short answer is sin. Since you already knew the short answer, let's talk about it in more detail.

> *"If you do what is right, will you not be accepted? But if you do not do what is right, sin is crouching at your door; it desires to have you, but you must rule over it." – Genesis 4:7*

The Apostle Paul understood the battle against sin that rages within those who seek godliness and wrote:

> *"As it is, it is no longer I myself who do it, but it is sin living in me. For I know that good itself does not dwell in me, that is, in my sinful nature. For I have the desire to do what is good, but I cannot carry it out. For I do not do the good I want to do, but the evil I do not want to do—this I keep on doing. Now if I do what I do not want to do, it is no longer I who do it, but it is sin living in me that does it. So I find this law at work: Although I want to do good, evil is right there with me." – Romans 7:17-21*

> *"What a wretched man I am!" – Romans 7:24*

Yes, we all are drawn to sin: *"For all have sinned and fall short of the glory of God, and all are justified freely by his grace through the redemption that came by Christ Jesus"* (Romans 3:23, 24).

When we come to Christ Jesus seeking forgiveness, the grace of God redeems us. As Christians, we become right with God because of Jesus. Our souls are secured in Christ and *nothing* can cancel the promise of eternal life we have with God, our Heavenly Father. I said *nothing!* Allow me to say it again, *NOTHING!*

However, this is just the beginning. We must grow and become more like Jesus, yet we are still drawn to sin. There are many reasons why we wrestle with sin. The war for our souls has been won by Jesus. However, the battle to keep us from growing in Christ, seeking godliness, and bearing fruit for the Kingdom of God continues.

The Apostle James wrote, *"Do not merely listen to the word, and so deceive yourselves. Do what it says. Anyone who listens to the word but does not do what it says is like someone who looks at his face in a mirror and, after looking at himself, goes away and immediately forgets what he looks like" (James 1:22-24).*

> Q. Why do we forget *what* we look like? First, we must answer: *who* do we begin to look like?

> *"To them God has chosen to make known among the Gentiles the glorious riches of this mystery, which is Christ in you, the hope of glory." – Colossians 1:27*

When we come to Jesus Christ, the Holy Spirit begins to transform us into His likeness. We become new creatures in Christ *(2 Corinthians 5:17)*. When we look into the mirror of our soul, we see that process of transformation.

So why do we forget what we look like? One truly fundamental reason is that this transformation process is painful. Growing closer to God means growing closer to His holiness. It is painful, and it takes courage to see yourself the way you truly are and to see all the selfishness and shame in the presence of a holy God. It is difficult to trust the Holy Spirit of God to work out our salvation (actually, our sanctification) at times in reverent fear and with trembling *(Philippians 2:12)*. Therefore, it is easier to simply walk away from the mirror and avoid the pain. However, when we look away from the mirror of our soul, we also forget what God has done in our life and how much we have grown closer to Him. We forget that truth when we must humble ourselves and turn from our wicked ways in order to find goodness and mercy *(2 Chronicles 7:14)*.

> *"Surely goodness and mercy shall follow me all the days of my life: and I will dwell in the house of the LORD forever." – Psalm 23:6*

I wondered for many years why David said that goodness and mercy would *follow* him all of his days. Then I remembered. David was a man of God who understood that he was prone to sin and disobedience toward God. He also understood that, if he had the *guts* to turn back toward God and seek forgiveness, he would find God's goodness and mercy. It takes *guts* to come before a holy God and allow the Spirit of God to work Himself in our lives to create godliness and make us more like Jesus. Do you have that kind of *guts*?

Standing Up

When we want to do what is right and be obedient to the will of God, we may find fear scratching at our door and demanding us to open up. It is fear that will whisper in our ear that we are not worthy to serve God, that we are ill-equipped, or that He will abandon us. Don't listen to it! The Bible warns against the temptation to yield toward fear in our heart. Rather, we must master fear! How do we do this? Through faith in God *(Psalm 23:4)*. However, how do we have the faith to master sin? By looking for the fingerprints of God that remind us of His hand of faithfulness.

Getting Out of the Way

Once we begin to exercise our faith in God and master fear in a particular situation, we see *God's faithfulness.* However, it won't take long before comfort sets in. Before you know it, we lose our sensitivity to our dependency on God. The healthy, reverent fear of being alone apart from God and needing to be dependent upon God may quickly become replaced by complacency. Then look out—pride will soon rise up! We may find ourselves trying to *sideline and bench* the Holy Spirit by saying, "That's alright. I got this one." Sounds innocent enough, right? *Wrong!*

How do we master the temptation toward pride? We must be vigilant in maintaining our dependency on God *(Psalm 23:3)*. How do we practice vigilance in maintaining our dependency on God to master sin? Through daily training in spiritual discipline resulting in humility because of repentance and a pure heart.

Sitting Down When It's Time

"Anyone who runs ahead and does not continue in the teaching of Christ does not have God; whoever continues in the teaching has both the Father and the Son." – 2 John 1:9

Q. Why would someone run ahead of God?

When we *walk* in obedience according to God's will, He showers us with His blessings because our focus is on His will. However, it can become very dangerous when our focus shifts to seeking God's blessings. Seeking the blessing at the expense of the Blesser is yielding to temptation and opening our heart to want (lust or greed). How do we master want? The antidote to want is *maintaining our gratitude* for what God has done for us *(Psalm 23:1, 2)*. However, how do we maintain our contentment and gratitude toward God? Is there hope for living a godly life in a world where sin continually saturates our eyes, such as the lure of instant gratification and rebellion toward the things of God?

We see the root to our sin is *temptation*. The Apostle James is very clear regarding temptation and we see this law of sin and death working within us.

"When tempted, no one should say, 'God is tempting me.' For God cannot be tempted by evil, nor does he tempt anyone; but each person is tempted when they are enticed and dragged away by their own evil desire and enticed. Then, after desire has conceived, it gives birth

*to sin; and sin,-when it is full-grown, gives birth
to death." – James 1:13-15*

The only way we truly master want, as with all sin, is
through the Spirit of God.

Q. Why is my prayer life so weak at times?

Now you may see how essential the practice of mature
prayer is for God's will to fill our life. I hope you are
beginning to understand that the degree of weakness or
strength in our prayer life is directly related to our ability to
rule over sin (*Genesis 4:7*). As Christians, we yield to
temptation because of the lack of spiritual discipline in our
life.

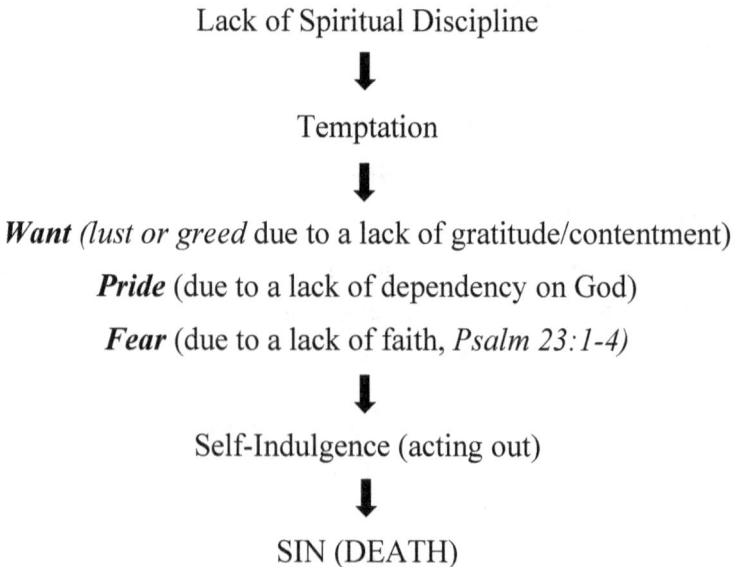

Lack of Spiritual Discipline

⬇

Temptation

⬇

Want *(lust or greed* due to a lack of gratitude/contentment)

Pride (due to a lack of dependency on God)

Fear (due to a lack of faith, *Psalm 23:1-4)*

⬇

Self-Indulgence (acting out)

⬇

SIN (DEATH)

Beware! Want says, "I must have it!" Pride says, "I deserve it." Fear says, "I do not believe God."

Now you see how easy it is to do the will of God—simply master sin! How do we do *that*? Again, it is only through spiritual discipline that we place ourselves in a position where the Holy Spirit of God can work in our life to draw us closer to Jesus. *When* we do this, there is no place for sin in our lives. Notice, I said *when* we do this. There will always be a battle waging within the members of our soul. However, our strength, promise, and victory is in Jesus!

> *"No, in all these things we are more than conquerors through him who **loved** us." –*
> *Romans 8:37*

Q. How do we develop a stronger life in Prayer?

Through spiritual discipline! A weak prayer life, due to a lack of spiritual discipline, must never be confused with the barriers and hindrances associated with *spiritual forces of evil in heavenly realms (Daniel 10:12-13; Ephesians 6:12).*

We will see later in this book that anything we do that causes growth toward Jesus and pleases our Heavenly Father is a result of obedience to the Holy Spirit. But where does that ability to obey come from? It comes from *love*—not from a love *for* God, but from the love *of* God.

Sacrifice and obedience from a love *for* God is offered from within and generated from our own heart independent from the Spirit of God and His love. Soon, the mechanics of obedience generated without the love *of* God attempts to generate a love *for* God from within our own heart. This futile effort to obtain the pure love *of* God in our own strength is self-righteousness and labeled collectively as religion.

However, the love *of* God comes from the Spirit of God. It is a gift. It cannot be generated from within our heart independent from the Spirit of God. It is not the goal of spiritual discipline to master the Spirit of God and somehow force God's love upon us or on others. When we try to master the spiritual realm independent from God and attempt to generate spiritual gifts and powers for our own selfish purposes, we are practicing witchcraft. It is the goal of spiritual discipline to prepare our heart and submit to the Spirit of God so He can bear fruit for the Kingdom of God, most specifically the love of God!

This Chapter's Prayer for You

Dear Heavenly Father, there is no God but You. There is no name above heaven or on earth greater than Yours. Give me the guts to overcome the pain of looking into Your mirror and seeing all the things in me that are displeasing to You. It is painful to see the selfishness and shame in me. Give me the courage to see myself the way I truly am in the presence of a Holy God and to trust the Holy Spirit of God to work out my salvation (more specifically, sanctification). Draw me closer to Jesus. Deliver me from evil. Show me how to master sin. Help me to develop a seasoned spiritual discipline so that I may overcome the temptation of want (lust, greed), pride, and fear. Teach me to be grateful and content. Help me to be totally dependent on You. Thank You for Your forgiveness, for securing my soul in Christ, and Your promise of eternal life. I thank You for continuing to work in me godliness that makes me more like Jesus. Amen.

God the Father's Promise to You

"And this is love: that we walk in obedience to his commands. As you have heard from the beginning, his command is that you walk in love." – 2 John 1:6

Questions for Next Chapter

1. Is there a right way to pray?
2. Is it selfish to pray for your own needs?
3. Why should we pray for others?
4. When should we pray?

Chapter 10
How Do We Pray?

Our heart is the barometer that gauges what we believe is right. Spiritual discipline calibrates our barometer to the righteousness that comes from Christ.

This Chapter's Questions:

1. Is there a right way to pray?
2. Is it selfish to pray for your own needs?
3. Why should we pray for others?
4. When should we pray?

What has God shown you so far in preparing for this chapter after reviewing these questions?

Q. Is there a right way to pray?

Anyone who has been in a car and verbalized the name of Jesus before narrowly avoiding a major accident knows that if prayer requires specific components, spoken in a specific order, all our insurance premiums would be much higher! So, is there a right way to pray? No. However, circumstances should never dictate our understanding, or our attempt to grasp a better understanding, when it comes to the things of God. So too it is with prayer.

This guidebook is far from being an exhaustive effort to encapsulate the grand mystery of prayer. Likewise, this chapter is far from being an exhaustive sermon on how to pray. There are many wonderful literary works written by learned Christian scholars on how to pray. Many authors and teachers of the Bible agree that when we study how to pray, who best to start with than Jesus?

For most, the journey on how to pray begins with the Lord's Prayer. In addition, we see Jesus' practical example of how to pray for Himself and for others in the Gospel of John, chapter 17. In the Gospel of Matthew, chapter 26 (also *Mark 14:32-42* and *Luke 22:39-46*), we see Jesus' intense prayer of obedience and submission to God the Father in the Garden of Gethsemane. Let us take a closer look at these three examples from Jesus' life.

In the Gospel of Matthew, chapter 6, verses 9-13 (also *Luke 11:2-4*) we have the Lord's Prayer. In these passages of Scripture, Jesus teaches the basic framework for Prayer.

"This, then, is how you should pray: Our Father in heaven, hallowed be your name, your kingdom come, your will be done, on earth as it is in heaven. Give us today our daily bread. And forgive us our debts, as we also have forgiven our debtors." – Matthew 6:9-12

"And lead us not into temptation, but deliver us from evil: For thine is the kingdom, and the power, and the glory, forever. Amen" – Matthew 6:13, KJV

Prayer Framework Part 1 - Our Relationship to God the Father and a Salutation

Our prayers should start with a salutation to the Holy One, the Creator of Heaven and Earth. This relationship is what separates Christianity from other religions and philosophies. You can gain some understanding into a particular faith or religion by its prayer format. As Christians, Jesus is reminding us that we are children of the Most High. We must never forget our God is a God of relationship. There are few, if any, higher priorities for our Heavenly Father. We see this example of salutation and establishment of relationship throughout Apostle Paul's epistles and the other Apostles' letters of the New Testament.

Prayer Framework Part 2 - Acknowledgment of God's Sovereignty

I find it very interesting and believe it extremely important to note, that Jesus emphases the importance of acknowledging Who God is and His sovereign will. This is a foundational truth, not only for answered prayer, but the ultimate purpose of prayer as a spiritual discipline that draws us closer to Jesus. In the Garden of Gethsemane, Jesus gave us a practical example of yielding to the sovereign will of God *(Mark 14:35-36)*. Jesus taught us to trust in the sovereignty of God and His purpose for our life and allowing the Holy Spirit to accomplish that through our spiritual discipline!

Q. Is it selfishness to pray for your own needs?

The fact that this is an honest question for many Christians is an indication of the influence in the church of the world's warped understanding of Christianity. This is the result of poor teaching of the Bible and an attack by evil to hinder the prayers of the believer. Throughout the Holy Scriptures, we see instructions and examples of praying for oneself.

Prayer Framework Part 3 – Specific Needs

In the Lord's Prayer, Jesus taught, *"Give us today our daily bread" (Matthew 6:11)*. Jesus clearly taught us that not only is it permissible to pray for oneself, but that it should be part of a healthy lifestyle.

> *"And will not God bring about justice for his chosen ones, who cry out to him day and night? Will he keep putting them off?" – Luke 18:7*

Praying for our personal daily needs declares a dependency upon God for everything, including our daily bread. In addition, when we pray for our daily needs, we are disciplining ourselves to not take God's provisions for granted.

Jesus not only taught us how to pray, He gave us practical examples of how to pray. On the night before He was betrayed, Jesus prayed for His disciples, all believers, and eventually for Himself after His Last Supper *(John 17:1-5)* and in the Garden of Gethsemane *(Luke 22:39-44* and *Matthew 26:36-46)*.

God's promises are His Word. For example:

> *"As the rain and the snow come down from heaven, and do not return to it without watering the earth and making it bud and flourish, so*

that it yields seed for the sower and bread for the eater, so is my word that goes out from my mouth: It will not return to me empty, but will accomplish what I desire and achieve the purpose for which I sent it. You will go out in joy and be led forth in peace; the mountains and hills will burst into song before you, and all the trees of the field will clap their hands. Instead of the thornbush will grow the juniper, and instead of briers the myrtle will grow. This will be for the Lord's renown, for an everlasting sign, that will endure forever." – Isaiah 55:10-13

God's promises are opportunities to exercise our faith and to believe God. However, God's Word, including His promises, will not return void. Consider the following passage of Scripture:

"Jesus replied: 'A certain man was preparing a great banquet and invited many guests. At the time of the banquet he sent his servant to tell those who had been invited, "Come, for everything is now ready." But they all alike began to make excuses. The first said, "I have just bought a field, and I must go and see it. Please excuse me." Another said, "I have just bought five yoke of oxen, and I'm on my way to try them out. Please excuse me." Still another said, "I just got married, so I can't come." The servant came back and reported this to his

master. Then the owner of the house became angry and ordered his servant, "Go out quickly into the streets and alleys of the town and bring in the poor, the crippled, the blind and the lame." "Sir," the servant said, "what you ordered has been done, but there is still room." Then the master told his servant, "Go out to the roads and country lanes and compel them to come in, so that my house will be full. I tell you, not one of those who were invited will get a taste of my banquet."'" – Luke 14:16-23

In this passage above, the refused invitation went to someone else. Likewise, as in *Isaiah 55:10-13*, the Word of God is never spoken in vain. His promises will not return empty if refused or not believed by someone. They will simply remain valid until their purpose is accomplished when someone has faith, receives the invitation or promise, and acts on or upon it.

Read what Queen Esther was told when she was to obey God:

"Do not think that because you are in the king's house you alone of all the Jews will escape. For if you remain silent at this time, relief and deliverance for the Jews will arise from another place, but you and your father's family will perish. And who knows but that you have come to your royal position for such a time as this?" – Esther 4:13, 14

We are to exercise our faith to act upon the promises of God through spiritual discipline such as prayer. Please read and consider the book of Hebrews, chapters 4 and 5. In this section of the Holy Scriptures, the author spoke of the Promised Land and the promise of rest God gave to the Hebrew people when they were in the desert. However, it was because of disobedience, but even more so of fear and a lack of faith, that caused the Hebrew people to refuse God's invitation or promise.

> *"For we also have had the good news proclaimed to us, just as they did; but the message they heard was of no value to them, because they did not share the faith of those who obeyed." – Hebrews 4:2*

The author of the book of Hebrews referred to this rest as a Sabbath Rest or a holy rest set apart for God. The good news is that this promise from God of rest, a Sabbath Rest, for the people of God still remains!

> *"Therefore, since the promise of entering his rest still stands, let us be careful that none of you be found to have fallen short of it." – Hebrews 4:1*

> *"Therefore since it still remains for some to enter that rest, and since those who formerly had the good news proclaimed to them did not go in because of their disobedience." – Hebrews 4:6*

"There remains, then, a Sabbath-rest for the people of God." – Hebrews 4:9

Q. So, now I ask you, are we to pray for ourselves?

I hope your answer is a resounding *yes* and *amen!* God has given specific promises to you and to me. All of these promises come from God's promise of life. That promise of life is only in Jesus.

"The thief comes only to steal and kill and destroy; I have come that they may have life, and have it to the full." – John 10:10

As with all of the Word of God, these promises will not return to God void. We are to believe every one of our promises of life and provision. Through the obedience we gain from the love of God, we are able to proclaim our faith at the throne of God's grace. We do this as God's priests through prayer to our Great High Priest, Jesus. The Word of God and His promise is clear. However, if we do not receive and act upon it, the promise will move on to someone who will. *We must never neglect* to walk in obedience through faith and offer our personal prayers according to His promises. Whether due to ignorance, presumption, or self-righteousness, doing so is eventually disastrous.

"Be always on the watch, and pray that you may be able to escape all that is about to happen, and that you may be able to stand before the Son of Man." – Luke 21:36

Therefore, praying for ourselves and believing God, His Word, and His promises, are not only permissible, but is an essential component in our relationship with Jesus our Lord and God our Father.

Prayer Framework Part 4 – Conclusion with Acknowledgement of God's Supremacy

The Garden of Gethsemane was Jesus' finest hour. Please consider carefully the following passage of Scripture:

> *"Jesus went out as usual to the Mount of Olives, and his disciples followed him. On reaching the place, he said to them, 'Pray that you will not fall into temptation.' He withdrew about a stone's throw beyond them, knelt down and prayed, 'Father, if you are willing, take this cup from me; yet not my will, but yours be done.' An angel from heaven appeared to him and strengthened him. And being in anguish, he prayed more earnestly, and his sweat was like drops of blood falling to the ground." – Luke 22:39-44*

Did Jesus sweat blood? Possibly, or this verse of Scripture may simply be a metaphor. What is important to understand is the torturous intensity of His prayer.

Q. Why was Jesus's prayer so intense that His sweat was like blood?

Q. What was Jesus praying *for* in the Garden of Gethsemane at the Mount of Olives?

Q. Did He not know the will of God?

Q. Was Jesus appealing to the heart of God the Father and praying that He would change His mind?

Q. Was this a prayer of petition (a request from someone) or a prayer of intercession (an intervention to change something)?

Q. On the other hand, was Jesus, as a man, asking God the Father to change His (Jesus) heart and strengthen Him through His prayer?

Jesus, in this moment as a man, was openly and honestly baring His heart to God the Father and expressing His battle with the flesh—His human condition. Jesus acknowledged that His human will needed to be in alignment with God the Father's will. His focus was not on the answer to His prayer, as much as seeking a change in His own human heart through the power of His prayer and the Holy Spirit within Him. We must never forget that the answers to our prayers are God's domain. Our personal growth and walk or *sanctification* is our domain!

Q. Is it ever acceptable to say no to our Heavenly Father?

Consider the Parable of the Two Sons:

"What do you think? There was a man who had two sons. He went to the first and said, 'Son, go and work today in the vineyard.' 'I will not,' he answered, but later he changed his mind and went. Then the father went to the other son and

said the same thing. He answered, 'I will, sir,'
but he did not go. Which of the two did what his
father wanted?" – Matthew 21:28-30

Q. So, what do *you* think? Why do you think the first
son changed his mind and obeyed his father?

Jesus goes on to explain the parable by saying those
who by *nature* refused God by saying no were received by
God after they repented.

Jesus gives us an example in the Garden of
Gethsemane on the purpose and wonderful power of prayer.
Our prayers must always begin with an open and honest heart
before our God the Father. That may mean saying, "No, no,
no!" to God while in prayer.

The purpose of every prayer must result in the freedom
of the Holy Spirit to accomplish God's will. Although our
spirit may be willing—knowing, obeying, submitting to, and
doing the will of God the Father—these things are impossible
to accomplish in our own strength or flesh *(Matthew 26:41).*
On the contrary, our flesh is always opposed and at war with
the will of God. It cannot submit to it. Just as the angel
strengthened Jesus, we need the Holy Spirit working in our life
to overcome our flesh and for our will to line up with the will
of God our Father.

When temptation appears overwhelming and our flesh
battles our spirit for our very soul, it is in the Garden of
Gethsemane that we hear Jesus saying, "I know, I know."
When we are weary and heavily burdened by the trials of this
world, we can turn to Jesus knowing, that as a man, He

experienced every fiery arrow, every propensity to want, pride and fear from the evil one as we do. Yet, He did not fail; He did not sin.

> *"Therefore, since we have a great high priest who has ascended into heaven, Jesus the Son of God, let us hold firmly to the faith we profess. For we do not have a high priest who is unable to empathize with our weaknesses, but we have one who has been tempted in every way, just as we are—yet he did not sin. Let us then approach God's throne of grace with confidence, so that we may receive mercy and find grace to help us in our time of need." –* Hebrews 4:14-16

True prayer results in a change within us. We establish the full power of prayer in our life through the Spirit of God and spiritual discipline, although we may believe it is a need that brings us to our knees in prayer. It is when we finally say yes and surrender to God and His will that we truly receive a change in our heart. That is how we grow closer to Jesus!

Q. Why should we pray for others?

1. For protection. In *John 17:11-12, 15,* Jesus prays for His disciples.
2. For believer unity. In *John 17:20-26,* Jesus prays for other believers.
3. For God's love (*John 17:26*).
4. So that others will believe and see God's existence, power and will for their salvation!

Consider the story of Jesus raising Lazarus from the dead (*John 11:39-44, especially v. 40*).

> Q. What was it that Jesus told Martha to believe *(John 11:25)*? What did Jesus pray? For the people to believe in Him!

Q. When Should We Pray?

> Q. What did Paul mean by *'pray continually'*? *(1 Thessalonians 5:17).*

> Q. *"And when you pray, do not keep on babbling like pagans, for they think they will be heard because of their many words" (Matthew 6:7).* Was Jesus commending the Jewish leaders of that time for their repetitiously, ceremonial prayers before men? No. The Apostle Paul encouraged us to continually stay sensitive to the Holy Spirit, through prayer, that we might know the will of God.

"For this reason, since the day we heard about you, we have not stopped praying for you. We continually ask God to fill you with the knowledge of his will through all the wisdom and understanding that the Spirit gives" – Colossians 1:9

This Chapter's Prayer for You

Dear God, You are the Holy One, the Creator of Heaven and Earth. All glory, honor and praise belongs to You. You alone are worthy and all creation displays its worship to

You. I know You hear my daily prayers of personal needs as I declare my dependency upon You for everything, even my daily bread. Help me to believe every one of Your promises of life and provision, not only for me, but for all those I pray for. Keep me focused so that I never forget the need that brings me to my knees in prayer is my opportunity to surrender to You and Your will. Let that truly change my heart so that I may grow closer to You, Jesus!

God the Father's Promise to You

> *"Create in me a pure heart, O God, and renew a steadfast spirit within me. Do not cast me from your presence or take your Holy Spirit from me. Restore to me the joy of your salvation and grant me a willing spirit, to sustain me." –*
> *Psalms 51:10-12*

Next Chapter's Question:

1. Who do we pray to?

Chapter 11
Who Do We Pray To?

When you cannot see the hand of God in your present, look for His fingerprints in you past!

This Chapter's Question:

1. Who do we pray to?

We started this study wrestling with the question of who God is. We acknowledged that God is too great, too powerful, unfathomable, and incompressible to define. He is omnipotent, omniscient, and omnipresent.

> *"But we do see Jesus"* (Hebrews 2:9). Jesus is God! Jesus shared divine glory with God the Father. *"And now, Father, glorify me in your presence with the glory I had with you before the world began." – John 17:5*

When Jesus walked this earth, crowds of people came to Him and many followed Him.

Q. Why did the people come to Jesus?

Was it because he was tall, dark, and handsome? Maybe He wore the latest fashion in fine clothes and was adorned with precious jewels. No, actually, the Bible says, *"He had no beauty or majesty to attract us to him, nothing in his appearance that we should desire him" (Isaiah 53:2).* Yes, Jesus did perform great miracles, many of them early in His three-year ministry. Yet, the people continued to come to Jesus even when He answered them by saying, *"A wicked and adulterous generation asks for a sign! But none will be given it except the sign of the prophet Jonah" (Matthew 12:39).* Why?

It was the words of Jesus, the very Word of God that attracted people to Him.

> *"In the beginning was the Word, and the Word was with God, and the Word was God. He was with God in the beginning." – John 1:1, 2*

> *"The Word became flesh and made his dwelling among us." – John 1:14*

It was the words of Jesus that spoke to the broken condition of the people's heart at that time, and it is still true today. There were those who heard Jesus speak to every aspect of the wretched reality concerning the state of this fallen world and were blessed by God.

> *"Come, see a man who told me everything I ever did. Could this be the Messiah?" – John 4:29*

I think it makes us a little nervous to reflect and meditate on the humanity of Jesus, the Son of Man. We see this in movies where the image of Jesus is portrayed larger than life, along with His glory and divinity of everything He did. This mindset cannot be further from the truth.

> *"For this reason he had to be made like them, fully human in every way, in order that he might become a merciful and faithful high priest in service to God, and that he might make atonement for the sins of the people. Because he himself suffered when he was tempted, he is able to help those who are being tempted." –*
> *Hebrews 2:17, 18*

Everything Jesus did, every miracle, even His death on a cross, He did by total obedience, submission, and reliance on God the Father through the Holy Spirit of God. He developed these acts throughout the years, as a man, because of His spiritual discipline, such as prayer and fasting. Therefore, we find Jesus fulfilling the sovereign will of God. He accomplished this by living His life as an example of holiness and righteous living. However, this is not the Jesus we pray to.

The Jesus that walked this earth died as a man. However, the Jesus we know, preach, and live for, rose from the grave and ascended to heaven. This Jesus now sits at the right hand of God the Father with all of the glory He once had.

> *"And now, Father, glorify me in your presence with the glory I had with you before the world began." – John 17:5*

God the Son has been reconciled to God the Father and now we are reconciled to God the Father because of the work of God the Son, Jesus. This is the message of good news found in the Gospels that brings us hope, strengthens our faith, and is the foundation of our salvation.

Q. Who do we pray to?

It is this Jesus, our risen Lord and King, arrayed in splendor and glorified as God that we pray to as our Great High Priest.

> Q. What is the difference between the glorified Jesus, God the Son—Who sat at the right hand of God the Father before separating from His glory and came to walk among men—and the glorified Jesus, God the Son—Who was raised from the dead and *now* sits at the right hand of God the Father?

> *"For we know that if the earthly tent we live in is destroyed, we have a building from God, an eternal house in heaven, not built by human hands. Meanwhile we groan, longing to be clothed instead with our heavenly dwelling." –* 2 Corinthians 5:1, 2

> *"Then he said to Thomas, 'Put your finger here; see my hands. Reach out your hand and put it into my side. Stop doubting and believe.'"* – John 20:27

> Q. When we are clothed with our heavenly dwelling, or heavenly bodies, will they be marred by the same deformities, scars, and disfigurements we now possess? I think not.

Our glorified Lord, Jesus, is the same yesterday, today, and tomorrow, except for His glorified body. Among those with glorified bodies, only Jesus' body bears the scars of an earthly life and death *(John 20:26, 27)*. Jesus' dying on the Cross, the prints left by the nails driven into our Lord's hands and feet, and the gaping wound in His side from the soldier's sword will for eternity remind us of the ultimate sacrifice Jesus paid, as a man, for our redemption. Additionally, *"For we do not have a high priest who is unable to empathize with our weaknesses, but we have one who has been tempted in every way, just as we are- yet he did not sin" (Hebrews 4:15 John 20:26, 27)*.

This is the Jesus that we pray to. The wounds remind us of Jesus in the Garden of Gethsemane where He wrestled with His humanity and prayed three times. He probably battled pride, want, and fear. He has overcome and won the victory. These wounds remind us that Jesus truly knows the pain of every battle we find ourselves combating every day. Even more so *when* we fail and fall short of His glory, we find His arms with these visible wounds reached out wide with healing.

> *"But he was pierced for our transgressions, he was crushed for our iniquities; the punishment that brought us peace was on him, and by his wounds we are healed." – Isaiah 53:6*

Notice in the Scripture above that it says, *"are healed,"* in the present tense. Jesus will never reject someone who desires to repent, walk with a pure heart, and has a steadfast faith. We may find this truth increasing as we grow and walk with Jesus. In fact, this may be a sign that we are growing closer to Jesus. The mature Christian is not one who does not sin, on the contrary, *"For all have sinned and fall short of the glory of God" (Romans 3:23).* The mature Christian is someone who, through spiritual discipline, like prayer and meditation on the Scriptures, is sensitive to the gentle wooing of the Spirit of God and runs quickly to those open arms of Jesus.

> *"Now Joshua was dressed in filthy clothes as he stood before the angel. The angel said to those who were standing before him, 'Take off his filthy clothes.' Then he said to Joshua, 'See, I have taken away your sin, and I will put fine garments on you.'" – Zechariah 3:3, 4*

We must never fall prey to the lie that we can cleanse ourselves solely by our own efforts. When we dismiss the voice of the Spirit of God and attempt to present ourselves as clean and pure before a Holy God, our efforts and works are in vain because of pride. When we do this, we also dismiss the gift of life through the work of Jesus and consider with contempt the one and only acceptable sacrifice, the blood of the Lamb.

The priesthood of Aaron in the Old Testament was under the Law of Moses. The priests were to ceremonially wash and cleanse themselves before serving, worshiping, and entering God's presence in the Most Holy Place. As priests of our Great High Priest, Jesus, we must understand that no amount of ceremonial washing or any other work apart from God will ever cleanse us enough to stand before a Holy God. Any attempt to do this is contempt for the work accomplished by Jesus. His ultimate sacrifice for our redemption means He was nailed to a cross and shed His holy and pure blood! It is only through spiritual discipline that we can totally obey, submit, and rely on our Heavenly Father. This spiritual discipline must be led, guided, and powered by the Holy Spirit of God. Only then can we rely on our Heavenly Father because of the work of Jesus, our Lord and Savior.

There now, we have come full circle—back to where we began: *back to Jesus!*

This Chapter's Prayer for You

Dear Heavenly Father God, to You be all glory and honor in heaven above and the earth below. Thank You, God, for Jesus, Who has been reconciled to You, and now we are reconciled to You because of the work of Jesus.

To You, Dear Jesus, our risen Lord and King, we acknowledge You as the Christ, the Anointed One arrayed in splendor and glorified as God in every way. You were from the beginning as the Word of God, have been with God, and is God. You sit at the right hand of God the Father. You became a man and made Your dwelling among us so that we might be right with God our Father. We pray to You as our Great High Priest.

Teach us to totally obey, submit, and rely on God the Father through the Holy Spirit of God. Give us a faithfulness in spiritual discipline to fulfill the sovereign will of God and live a life of righteous holiness. Most of all, pour Your love out upon us so that we may become more like You in all we do. In Jesus' name we pray!

God the Father's Promise to You

"And now, Father, glorify me in your presence with the glory I had with you before the world began." – John 17:5

Chapter 12
Concluding Thoughts

Jesus' truths and principles are unchangeable. Yet they are like musical notes. They are given uniquely by the Holy Spirit as the melody of our life's song to praise and worship our loving God.

⸺⸺⸺⸺⸺⸺⸺⸺⸺⸺⸺⸺⸺

Congratulations! You now know the: who, what, why, where, when and how elements of prayer. So now what?

The Apostle Paul wrote in 1 Corinthians 13:1-3, *"If I speak in the tongues of men or of angels, but do not have love, I am only a resounding gong or a clanging cymbal. If I have the gift of prophecy and can fathom all mysteries and all knowledge, and if I have a faith that can move mountains, but do not have love, I am nothing. If I give all I possess to the poor and give over my body to hardship that I may boast, but do not have love, I gain nothing."*

Without God's love, we not only have nothing of true value, we are *tempted* to believe we *are* nothing of true value. Although God honors the prayers of those who pray for us, ultimately, only you can choose to receive the power that makes long-lasting meaningful change in your life.

What does this really mean? We have discussed the importance of exercising a daily practice of spiritual discipline.

In addition to prayer's impact upon your life, we looked at the necessity of prayer for communion with the Holy Spirit and intercession for others, meditation in the Holy Scriptures, journaling, and fasting. However, only through the pursuit of *His* love will you be the person God the Father created you to be.

It is the love of God the Father found in Jesus Christ that causes meaningful change in our life. Only God's love, expressed through His Holy Spirit, imparts to us the power to choose forgiveness when abused, safeguard peace when surrounded by despair, have patience when dismissed, offer kindness in response to cruelty, show goodness when dishonored, allow faith to master fear, convey gentleness when rejected, present mercy when falsely accused, and display joy when your heart breaks. *(Remember Galatians 5:22?)*

Only you have the power to look up, get up, and walk when Jesus says to you, *"Come, follow me..." (Matthew 4:19a).*

Today your sails have been dropped.

The wind is at your back.

The Word of God is now your map.

There is nothing that you lack.

Your destination is now clear.

Tomorrow is not known,

But the rudder is in your hands,

And Jesus is your own!

Did you enjoy this book?

Has it helped you in your quest for the truth and the love of God?

If so, please consider spreading this message by writing a review on www.amazon.com so that others may enjoy its fruit.

Thank you for your support of this ministry.

For more information on the author, other books, and seminars, go to:

www.bubblingspringsbooks.com

About the Author

And the LORD answered me: "Write the vision; make it plain on tablets, so he may run who reads it." –
Habakkuk 2:2, ESV

❖———————————————————❖

Sam has had several ministries during his walk with Christ. He received an Honorable Discharge after serving in the military for four years and then attended college in Los Angeles, California. After 8 years, he earned several degrees including a doctorate in chiropractic. It was during his time in Chiropractic College that Sam came to Jesus because of the fervent prayers of Christians who would not take no for an answer.

For 13 years, Sam practiced at Barone Christian Chiropractic Family Center in Pittsburgh Pennsylvania with his lovely wife Peggy. They served the body of Christ as well as the lost. The number of miracles performed by the mighty hand of God and witnessed by Dr. Sam and his patients are too numerous to count. It was also during this time that Dr. Sam began to receive some understanding of God's sovereignty. Sometimes God would answer prayers for healing by calling patients to their heavenly home.

While maintaining a full-time practice, Dr. Sam received formal training in God's Word through attending Greater Works Bible College in Monroeville, Pennsylvania. He also taught grade school at their academy.

In 2002, God called Sam and Peggy to Honolulu, Hawaii. While performing his duties as a Federal Investigator in the area of public health, he was, and still is, active in his local church, Pacific Islands Bible Church. He has presented messages on faith, worship, and Christian growth. At times, he and Peggy open their home to weekly small group Bible studies, where relationships such as marriage are strengthened through God's love. The focus of Sam's messages is growing closer to God by knowing Christ through the Holy Scriptures, revelation from the Spirit of God, and spiritual discipline.

It was in response to his pastor's request to teach a course on prayer that this study guide was created. It is Sam's hope, prayer, and expectation that, by faith, God's endless blessing, received through exercising spiritual disciplines, such as prayer and the study of the Holy Scriptures, will draw you closer to Christ and therefore to God the Father. Sam prays that the Father's love and His Holy Spirit's wisdom will give you a deeper understanding into why prayer is the answer that propels us into a closer walk with Christ!

Sam and Peggy are transitioning to a life of fulltime RV living. This new ministry is devoted to traveling the country and sharing the good news of a life with Jesus to the RV community in small group settings. This ministry will enable Sam to share his gift as a teacher of the Bible's fundamental truths in a refreshing and inspiring manner to the body of Christ in churches and gatherings of all sizes. Seminar information can be found at www.bubblingspringsbooks.com.

www.ingramcontent.com/pod-product-compliance
Lightning Source LLC
Chambersburg PA
CBHW020503030426
42337CB00011B/215